America and the Robber Barons

AMERICA AND THE ROBBER BARONS

1865 to 1913

Fon W. Boardman, Jr.

Henry Z. Walck, Inc.
A Division of
David McKay Company, Inc.
New York

Library of Congress Cataloging in Publication Data

Boardman, Fon Wyman, 1911–
   America and the robber barons, 1865 to 1913.

   Bibliography: p.
   Includes index.
   SUMMARY: Discusses the economic conditions in
the United States between 1865 and 1913 and those
financiers who prospered during that period.
   1. Capitalists and financiers–United States–
Biography.   2. United States–Economic conditions–
1865–1918.   3. United States–History–1865–1918.
[1. United States–Economic conditions–1865–1918.
2. Capitalists and financiers].   I. Title.
HG172.A2B56   332'.092'4 [B]   79-11817
ISBN 0-8098-6000-7

10 9 8 7 6 5 4 3 2 1
Manufactured in the United States of America

For my very dear daughter
Constance Boardman DeMarco

Contents

1

The State of the Nation,
1865–1913

The Gilded Age, the Trusts, Muckrakers, and *Robber Barons*—
such words and phrases now belong to history. Not so long ago,
though, in terms of America's past, they aroused strong emotions,
touched off bitter debates, figured in controversial political
campaigns, and were linked to the causes of violent labor
disputes. They brought to the minds of millions of persons visions
of great wealth, of vast business enterprises doing as they wished
with the environment and the natural resources of a continent,
and of corruption widespread in city, state, and federal government, including the Congress of the United States.

These words referred to men and events that had a great deal
to do with shaping the United States we live in, even now in the
last quarter of the twentieth century. The years involved were,
roughly, the nearly half century from the end of the Civil War in
1865 to the early days of President Woodrow Wilson's administration in 1913. The period was one of great growth for the nation: in
population, in importance in world affairs, in science and invention, and in culture and education. The dominating aspect of the
nation's life and development was, however, economic: manufacturing, mining, transportation, communication, finance, business, technology, and agriculture.

No nation in history has changed more in half a century in the
form and scope of its economic life than did the United States.

And this change, which was one of both quantity and quality, in turn improved or damaged, helped or harmed all other aspects of the life of the nation and its people. If, for example, the new leaders of industry gave money to schools and churches, they also used their money to bribe legislators; if the railroads and factories they built contributed to the efficiency and comfort of life, they did so at the cost of permanent damage to the environment and hardship for hundreds of thousands of laborers.

Perhaps the most impressive aspect of this economic revolution was the appearance of a group of intelligent, energetic men, of immense ambition and practical ability, who became the leaders of the new industrial age. Unhampered by government restraints and operating in an age and atmosphere of low ethical standards in business, they acquired wealth and power far beyond the dreams of earlier Americans. Some of these men made lasting contributions to the economic strength of the nation; others used their talents merely to fleece fellow citizens of their money. They came to be called Robber Barons, and in this book is some account of the lives and achievements of the leading members of this group of formidable men.

When the Civil War came to an end, one distinct era of the nation's life ended and another began. Casualties had been heavy: more than six hundred thousand died on both sides and the surviving wounded brought the total number of casualties to about a million. The South was not only defeated, but its factories, railroads, and farms were in ruins. Two things, though, had been decided once and for all: slavery was abolished and the Union of the states was not to be broken. A bitter struggle developed between President Andrew Johnson and Congress as to the terms under which the eleven southern states that had seceded were to be readmitted to the Union. The problem was not resolved until long after Johnson's term ended in 1869. In fact, it was 1877 before the Reconstruction process ended and the last of the former Confederate states was readmitted to full membership in the Union.

In spite of the devastation of four years of war and the preoccupation—physically and emotionally—with it on the part of the men and women on both sides, the nation continued to grow, at least in the North and the West, during those tragic years. In 1860, the year before the struggle began, the nation counted almost 31.5 million inhabitants; ten years later the total had increased by a little over 7 million. The 1880 census showed that the 50-million mark had been passed, and by 1890 there were almost 63 million Americans. The pace increased: nearly 76 million persons in 1900 as a new century began; 92.25 million in 1910; and before the next census in 1920, the 100-million mark had been passed. The increase in population and the migration of people, both native-born and immigrants, over the continent was reflected in the admission of states to the Union. In 1865 there were thirty-six states; between then and 1912 twelve more were admitted, beginning with Nebraska in 1867 and ending with Arizona and New Mexico. This brought the total to forty-eight, comprising the entire continental expanse of the United States territory, except for Alaska, which was purchased from Russia in 1867.

The years between 1865 and 1913 were also marked by a strong, steady movement of the population from farm and rural areas to urban regions. In 1870 only 25.7 percent of the people lived in towns with a population of 2,500 or more. The percentage rose steadily: to 35.1 in 1890; to 39.7 in 1900; and to 45.7 in 1910. The next census showed that in the intervening ten years the urban population had, for the first time, come to exceed the rural. Some of this change was accounted for by the movement, especially of young people, from farms to cities, and a great deal of it by immigrants coming from abroad. Behind these movements lay the compelling economic force of industrialization, which drew people to the urban areas where there existed jobs in the new and expanding factories, banks, and business offices.

Some of the immigrants, who arrived in large numbers even during the Civil War and in still larger numbers thereafter, went west and became pioneer farmers. More of them, though, settled in the cities and provided cheap, unskilled labor for factories, or did the hard work of laying down railroad tracks as the lines pushed west. In 1865, for example, 248,000 immigrants arrived to make their homes in America; in 1890 the figure was 455,000; and in 1913 almost 1,200,000 arrived. In the course of the fifty years from 1870 to 1920, a total of 26,276,000 persons, mostly from Europe, emigrated to the United States. Some of them came to escape political or religious persecution, or military conscription, but the great majority, drawn by tales of the jobs and riches to be found in booming America, came to improve their living standards.

By reason of its history as a democracy, and the long debate in Congress between North and South over the issue of slavery, the nation was accustomed to giving politics a central place in its affairs and its attention. After the Civil War, however, politics and government took second place to the industrial and business life of the country. No longer was politics considered the best career nor political office the highest goal. The new model for Americans seeking power and status was the clever financier, the hard-driving industrialist and the builder of continental railroads.

The Republican party, whose attitude toward big business was extremely favorable, dominated the political scene. Between 1856, when James Buchanan was elected president, and 1912, when Woodrow Wilson won over a divided Republican party, only one Democrat occupied the White House. He was Grover Cleveland (1837–1908), elected to two non-consecutive terms in 1884 and 1892, and he was conservative enough in his attitude toward money, banking, and government regulation to satisfy most Republican businessmen.

It was, indeed, a Republican president, Theodore Roosevelt, in office from 1901 to 1909, who was the only president in that period to offer any serious opposition to the masters of big business and monopolies. The battle lines between the new business and banking interests, on the one hand, and the small businessmen and the farmers, mostly in the South and West, on the other hand, were most clearly drawn in the 1896 presidential election. When the votes were counted, though, William McKinley, the Republican candidate, supported by generous amounts of money contributed by business and industry, defeated William Jennings Bryan, the Democratic candidate who represented the agrarian and labor interests. The electoral college vote was 271 to 176.

In keeping with the spirit of continental and economic expansion, the United States in this period also expanded as a world power, along with the imperialistic nations of Europe as a ruler of colonies. The brief Spanish-American War, fought between April and August 1898, resulted in the freeing of Cuba from

Spanish rule and the acquisition by the United States of Puerto Rico in the Atlantic and the Philippine Islands in the Pacific. Not all the people of the latter welcomed their new ruler and a bitter guerilla war went on until 1901. In July 1898 the Hawaiian Islands were annexed by treaty. In 1903, President Roosevelt, having seen to it that a revolution to separate Panama from Colombia succeeded, also saw to it that the United States promptly signed a treaty with the new nation. The United States was given the right to build a canal across the Isthmus of Panama. The construction task was a formidable one, but the canal was completed and opened to shipping in 1914.

For a variety of reasons, it was an exciting half century in which to be alive in America, and for many persons the most fascinating arenas of action were business, industry, and finance.

2
The Wealth of the Nation, 1865–1913

The enormous growth and change in the American economy created a new class of wealthy and powerful individuals who built up and controlled the new large-scale enterprises. Before the Civil War, to amass $100,000 was to be rich. The number of persons with fortunes in excess of $1 million was small. Fur trading started John Jacob Astor (1763–1848) on the way to wealth, while most prewar fortunes were based on shipping, trading, and real estate. Now the nation entered a period when fortunes of more than $100 million were made and when success was found in railroads, in heavy industry, in mining, and in investment banking.

These fortunes belonged to the men at the peak of an economic pyramid that had a very solid base. First of all was the continental expanse itself, rich in natural resources and ready to be settled and exploited by a fast-growing population. The increasing population, in turn, provided a ready supply of labor and an ever bigger market for manufactured goods. No restrictive customs or laws prevented the men at the top, who seized their opportunities where they found them, from doing as they pleased with their property and their money.

Only a few statistics are needed to indicate the economic growth that had no rival elsewhere. In 1859, the gross value of manufactured goods was just under $2 billion. By the turn of the century, the figure reached $13 billion; by 1909 it was nearly $20 billion and still going up. In the same period, the number of wage earners employed by these blossoming enterprises increased from 1,300,000 to more than 6,000,000 and also continued to grow. The amount of capital invested increased about in proportion, while productivity—the amount of goods produced per man-hour of labor—also rose amazingly. New discoveries of metal ores—both precious and those used in manufacturing— added to the flow of wealth. The Comstock Lode in Nevada alone yielded $340 million worth of silver in the thirty years ending in 1890. The capital needed to build plants and railroads came partly from Europe, where there were thousands of bankers and others eager to invest in the riches of America. At home, investment banking and the stock exchange system grew along with the industries whose securities they sold by the millions to those who hoped to share in the almost certain profits.

The economic growth and the accumulation of fortunes were not confined to heavy industry. Retail merchandising became big business, too, when such men as Alexander T. Stewart in New York in 1862, John Wanamaker in Philadelphia in 1877, and Marshall Field in Chicago in 1881 opened large department stores, the forerunners of even larger chains. All three became millionaires through their astute merchandising. The British historian, diplomat, and observer of American life, James Bryce (1838–1922), wrote in the 1880's: "Trade and manufactures cover the whole horizon of American life far more than they do anywhere in Europe. They . . . are the main concern of the country, to which all others are subordinate."

The new economic world also owed a great deal to science, technology, and invention. Chemistry was developing in such a way that its findings had practical applications, as in the steel and oil industries. Inventions such as the air brake by George Westinghouse in 1869 had obvious applications that improved transportation systems. Most prolific of the inventors was Thomas A. Edison (1847–1931), whose first contribution to the spirit of the age was to improve the telegraph so that two messages could be sent in each direction at once over the same facilities. Edison's greatest contribution to business and industry, though, was to invent efficient ways of using electricity for power and light. He produced a workable incandescent light bulb in 1878 and in 1882 opened a power station in New York City which, within two years, was lighting 11,272 lamps. Steam was, at the time, and remained, the principal source of power for industry, but more and more of the needed power was supplied by electric motors, while electric lighting made it possible to work in the factory or office during the hours of darkness.

The application of new methods and techniques, together with the managerial skills and systems needed to operate a large, nationwide industry, are exemplified in the careers of Philip D. Armour (1832–1901) and Gustavus F. Swift (1839–1903). Each established a meat-packing house in Chicago to produce and distribute meat products on a large scale. They organized the work so that a minimum amount of time was spent making use of almost every part of an animal in some way. Swift pioneered in the use of refrigerator cars, a necessity if meat products were to be sent to distant markets. Both made good use of advertising techniques to sell their products. Working conditions were horrible, as Upton Sinclair made clear in his vivid novel *The Jungle* (1906), and in 1898 Swift was charged with selling tainted beef to the government during the Spanish-American War. But both men made fortunes. Small, local packers found it hard, if not impossible, to compete, while livestock growers had to accept the prices the large packers chose to pay for their animals.

To sell products on a large scale over a continent, to operate railroads spanning that continent, and to keep the people of such an expanse informed, fast means of communication were a necessity. The telegraph, invented in 1844, spread its wires rapidly and thousands of miles were strung in the latter part of the nineteenth century. The two coasts were first connected by telegraph in the fall of 1861. Business transactions between Europe and America were speeded up when, under the leadership of Cyrus W. Field (1819–92), the Atlantic cable was successfully completed in 1866. The first transatlantic link by wireless was established in 1901. Most useful of all in enabling business and industry to communicate at any moment was the invention of the telephone in 1876. Within four years, 34,000 miles of telephone wires were in use and by 1895 people in New York and Chicago could talk to each other. As early as 1900, 1,355,000 phones were in use and the American Telephone and Telegraph

Company was already a quarter-of-a-billion-dollar corporation. The number of phones reached 9,000,000 in 1915, and that same year transcontinental service between New York and San Francisco became a reality.

Of equal importance were the invention and development of machines that speeded up and reduced the cost of written communication, thereby making it easier to issue and receive information and instructions throughout large and diversified corporations. The typewriter, like the telephone, was invented in 1876 and soon workable machines were being manufactured in large quantities. The typewriter was also responsible for the introduction into business offices, on a large scale, of women workers, who could easily use such machines and who seemed more adept at typing than men. The linotype machine in 1884, and bigger and faster printing presses, made it possible to disseminate more information more quickly and more cheaply.

While railroads were the backbone of the transportation system, four other developments were of considerable significance, not only to the nation in general but also to business and industry. The steam locomotive was adapted to the operation of elevated railroads within cities, the first being put in operation in New York in 1870. Electric power entered the transportation field with the running of the first electric trolley in Richmond, Virginia, in 1888. Subways made their first appearance in 1904 in New York. These different means of rapid mass transit made it possible for thousands of workers to live far beyond walking distance of factory and office, a necessity as the number of workers and the size of factories and offices grew. Finally, near the end of the century, a number of inventors produced practical automobiles, using the gasoline-powered internal combustion engine. Although there were only four thousand autos in the United States in 1900, within fifteen years there were nearly a million. The auto not only increased the mobility of workers but it also created a whole new market for products of the steel and oil industries, among others.

Less tangible than technological advances, but just as important to the growth of large-scale manufacturing operations and the formation of monopolies was the corporate form of business organization. In earlier times, individuals, alone or as partners with other men, formed businesses, but as time went on and the size of operations grew, this kind of organization was unsatisfactory. It depended too much on the activities and fates of individuals and it made it impossible to raise the large amounts of capital needed by modern business. The corporate form allowed an organization to sell stock to the public to raise capital. At the same time, though, it was fairly easy for a small group to control enough of this stock so that the average stockholder had little say in how the officers and directors ran the business.

Even the corporate form by itself did not satisfy the new business leaders when faced with competition within their field of enterprise. As a result, there appeared in the mid-1870's the "pool" arrangement. The leading firms in, say, sugar manufacturing, would agree on prices to be charged the public so that all in the pool would be sure to turn a profit at the expense of the public. These pools depended on "gentlemen's agreements" and could not be enforced, so they seldom lasted long. One member of a pool usually decided it was to his advantage to break his word and undersell his fellow pool members. When courts declared certain pools illegal, corporation lawyers thought up a new scheme—the "trust." In this arrangement the men who controlled the companies involved deposited their stock with a group of trustees and received trust certificates in return. The trustees then ran all the companies as a unit. Since a trust usually had full control over an industry—or at least effectively dominated it—the term came to be used somewhat interchangeably with "monopoly."

Another method of controlling an industry and of getting around antimonopoly legislation was the formation of a holding company. Such companies became possible when some states passed laws allowing companies to hold the stock of other corporations. In the most active period of corporate mergers and acquisitions, from 1897 to 1904, the holding company was the favorite device. In that period, as part of industry's growth and mergers, more than $6 billion worth of securities were put on the market. During these same years, the number of business combinations grew from 12 to 305 and these firms controlled nearly 40 percent of the capital then invested in manufacturing. New giant corporations—whether called trusts or monopolies—existed in many fields, including oil, steel, rubber, tobacco, paper, and matches. Adding legal sanction to economic power, the Supreme Court in 1886 decided that the Fourteenth

Amendment, which became part of the Constitution in 1868 in an attempt to assure full citizenship rights for the recently freed blacks, protected corporations as well as individuals.

Charles Francis Adams (1835–1915), a member of the famous Adams family of Massachusetts, who had an unpleasant experience when he became involved with one of the new breed of railroad manipulators, commented on the situation. In *Chapters of Erie* he wrote: "Modern society has created a class of artificial beings who bid fair soon to be the masters of their creator. . . . The system of corporate life and corporate power . . . is ever grasping new powers, or insidiously exercising covert influence. Even now the system threatens the central government."

The new and booming industries, such as steel and oil, were merely following in the footsteps of the railroads, which were the first business organizations to operate on a large scale. In fact, until well into the first quarter of the twentieth century, the era could well be known as the age of the railroad. The Civil War gave impetus to railroad building by showing how the lines could be used to move men and materials quickly over large distances when coordinated management took hold. After the war, railroads began spreading out like fingers all over the trans-Mississippi west. In so doing, they brought in thousands of settlers, had a large part in driving the American Indians off their native plains, opened the path to rich mines, and decided where cities would rise by where they ran their tracks. On the one hand, their pioneering in technology and management aided other businesses, while the abuses of their economic power was a prime factor in the later imposition of government regulations of industry. Their continental-scale operations even resulted in the adoption of the now familiar standard time zones. The railroad, especially the locomotive (or "iron horse"), spelled romance in the late nineteenth century. Locomotives were given names and American boys wanted to be railway engineers, not astronauts.

The railroads' central place in American life is shown most clearly in terms of the thousands of miles of tracks added to the system in this half century. When the Civil War ended in 1865, there were 35,000 miles of railroad tracks in the entire country. Within five years another 18,000 miles were added. The 1880's set a record, never surpassed, of 71,000 miles in the decade. Although the pace of construction slowed, the total went on up to

254,000 miles in 1916, an all-time high, more trackage than existed in all of Europe. Most of the post-Civil War construction was west of the Mississippi and some of the tracks were put down too soon in relation to the size of the population. Often there was not enough freight or passenger business to make for profitable operation.

The dollar figures involved in the building and operating of the railroads are as impressive as the mileage statistics. The total capitalization of the roads rose from $2.5 billion in 1870, to $10 billion in 1890, and to $21 billion in 1916. Unfortunately for investors, these figures in many cases exceeded the sensible capitalization of the roads if related strictly to cost, value, and earning power. In about this same period, operating revenues rose from $300 million a year to $4 billion a year. And as mileage and capitalization increased, so did the number of employees: from 163,000 in 1870 to a peak of 1,700,000 in 1916.

One more statistic adds a final touch to the unique story of the building of America's railroad system. In many places, especially across the Great Plains and through the Rocky Mountains, private capital, understandably, was not willing to risk the full amount needed to lay the tracks. It was not, however, considered proper for the government to build and run the railroads, so the lines were subsidized by the grant of public lands to private companies. By the time the great building spree was over, the federal government had contributed 131,350,000 acres and some of the states nearly another 49,000,000. This almost unimaginable expanse was, unfortunately, often secured under false pretenses and the proceeds from many acres went into the pockets of railroad promoters rather than into sound construction.

As railroad mileage and usage increased, so did the technological and mechanical aspects of operation. Locomotives became more powerful and trains ran at faster speeds. Such developments called in turn for better safety devices such as block signal systems, automatic coupling units, steel rails, and iron and steel bridges to replace the wooden ones which were forever catching fire. More comfort and luxury were gradually introduced, especially noteworthy being the Pullman sleeping car, which made its first appearance in 1859 and, in even grander form, in 1864.

The railroads set up pools to share freight traffic and to establish profitable rates. Three western lines, in direct competition with each other, formed the "Iowa Pool" in 1870 and agreed that they would share the traffic equally. A pool of southern lines grew to include twenty-seven roads by 1877 and an even larger pool was made up of the trunk lines running between New York and Chicago. Besides engaging in pools to control traffic and rates, railroads sometimes participated in an even more unfair practice. Freight rates were publicly announced, but large or otherwise favored shippers secretly received a rebate of part of the rate. In general, rates were decided on the basis of how much the railroad in question could get. A line without competition charged very high rates; in some cases a shipper paid more for a short haul than others did for a long haul. All these tactics resulted in mounting protests, especially on the part of western farmers, and eventually led to government regulation of the lines.

As railroads and manufacturing organizations grew both physically and financially, the individual laboring man of the time became increasingly powerless to deal on anything like equal terms with his employer. He was further handicapped by the large labor supply, augmented every year by more immigrants, while improvements in technology and machinery meant less skill was needed to perform many tasks. Although labor unions were not new on the American scene in 1865, it was not until 1869 that a national organization of any consequence was founded. In that year, under the leadership of Uriah S. Stephens (1821–82), the Knights of Labor came into being. The Knights welcomed all laboring people, regardless of trade or craft, and grew steadily. Terence V. Powderly (1849–1924) replaced Stephens as head of the union in 1879 and led it in successful strikes in 1884 and 1885 against the large railroad systems. In 1886, however, when membership reached a high of 702,000, another railroad strike ended in failure. Other causes accelerated the decline of the Knights, who by 1893 numbered only 74,000. The American Federation of Labor, founded in 1881, then became the most important national organization. It was a federation of unions, most of which were composed of the members of a single craft or trade. Under the leadership of Samuel Gompers (1850–1924), the AFL had 225,000 members by 1890; 550,000 in 1900; and about 2,000,000 in 1914. Despite its growth, it was not able during the nineteenth century to deal with big business on an equal basis except in isolated cases. Most men continued to work long hours at low pay: as late as 1900 the average annual pay of a wage earner was only $490, while the average workweek was sixty hours.

Labor could not find much consolation in Supreme Court decisions of the time. In one decision in 1905, the court ruled invalid a New York State law limiting the maximum number of hours per week a baker could work. In 1908, however, the court upheld an Oregon law limiting the hours of work by women. That same year, the court applied the Sherman Antitrust Act to labor. It was decided in the Danbury Hatters' case that a secondary boycott organized by striking workers was a conspiracy in restraint of trade.

The strike seemed to be the only weapon available to labor, and strikes on a national scale, accompanied by violence, took place for the first time. The most destructive occurred in 1877 when many railroads, using the excuse of poor business conditions (although they were paying large dividends to stockholders) cut the wages of their workers. Men of the Baltimore and Ohio Railroad went on strike when a second wage cut was announced. Although federal troops were sent to Martinsburg, West Virginia, where the strike began, it spread rapidly over the country. Freight yards were seized and tracks blockaded. There were casualties on both sides when the militia and strikers fired on each other, while damage to the extent of $5 million was done to railroad property in Pittsburgh. Eventually army troops restored order and the strikers lost some of the public sympathy first shown them because of the violence. In less than a month, the strike was over and labor had little to show for it.

Organized labor also suffered in the public's estimation as a result of the Haymarket Square bombing in Chicago in May 1886. Labor unions were campaigning for the eight-hour day at the same time that violence erupted between strikers and strike breakers during a long strike against the McCormick Harvester Company. The police killed or wounded half a dozen people and this led to a call for a protest rally in Haymarket Square. The meeting was dominated by a group of anarchists and, as a large force of police arrived, a bomb exploded, fatally wounding seven of them and wounding sixty or more others. The public blamed the anarchists and, unfairly, linked them with the labor unions. It was never discovered who threw the bomb, but eight anarchists were condemned to death and four of them hanged.

Another bitter, violent strike occurred in 1894 and was a struggle between labor and George M. Pullman (1831–97) and his prosperous Pullman Palace Car Company. Blaming the depression that began that year, Pullman laid off 3,000 of his 5,800 workers and reduced the wages of the others. He did not, however, reduce rents in his wholly owned company town of Pullman, Illinois. The Pullman strikers asked the American Railroad Union to support it by refusing to move trains that included Pullman cars. Eugene V. Debs (1855–1926), head of the union and an outstanding figure in organized labor for many years, was reluctant to do so, but agreed to cooperate while doing his best to keep the strike a peaceful one. The railroads asked the government for aid, partly on the grounds that the strikers were interfering with the United States mails. President Cleveland obligingly sent troops to Chicago while the federal government applied to the courts for an injunction against the strikers. Infuriated by the biased manner in which the government took the railroad owners' side, the strikers resorted to violence in Chicago. Debs and others were arrested for violating the injunction, the strike was broken and the union destroyed, while the roads blacklisted the strikers and refused ever to hire them again.

When the United Mine Workers struck the anthracite coalfields in Pennsylvania in 1902, the man then in the White House, Theodore Roosevelt (1858–1919), attempted to mediate rather than send troops to side with the owners. The mines were owned for the most part by half a dozen railroads whose presidents refused to enter into negotiations with the union, which was led by its president, John Mitchell (1870–1919). The stubborn attitude of the owners was expressed by their spokesman, George F. Baer: "The rights and interests of the laboring man will be protected and cared for—not by the labor agitators, but by the Christian men to whom God in His infinite wisdom has given the control of the property interests of this country." Such an attitude lost the owners public sympathy but, when Roosevelt called a meeting of the two sides in Washington, the owners refused to talk to the union leaders. Roosevelt was furious and finally convinced the leading financier, J. P. Morgan, that he would be doing a service if he talked the owners into a reasonable attitude. A commission was then appointed by the president and in March

1903 its decision gave the mine workers a 10 percent raise in pay and reduced working hours, but did not grant the union official recognition.

The nation's farmers, like the industrial workers, felt strongly that they, too, were being denied a fair share of the material benefits of a booming economy. They complained, usually legitimately, that railroads and grain storage elevator owners charged them unreasonably high rates while manufacturers, shielded by high tariffs on imports, charged them high prices for their goods. Like the laboring man, the individual farmer was not in a strong position to compete with the trusts and monopolies. Nevertheless, the number of farmers, farm acreage, and farm production all increased on a scale in keeping with the national growth in general. At the start of the period, farmers were just beginning to move into the Great Plains, where they later discovered that in many years there was not enough rainfall to permit the practice of farming as carried on in the East. After the 1890 census, its director declared that the western frontier no longer existed, thanks largely to the rapid invasion of farmers, both native-born and immigrant, joined also by thousands of miners. The South had to reorganize its agriculture without slaves, which it did at least so far as the size of the cotton crop was concerned: by 1875, 4.6 million bales were produced, compared with a low of 299,000 in 1865. In the Southwest, especially in Texas, cattle raising on a large scale ushered in the heyday of the legendary cowboy and the long cattle drives from Texas to railheads in Kansas.

In spite of the hazards of weather and the obstacles placed by railroads and trusts, American farmers not only grew in numbers but also in the value of their holdings. In 1880 all property of the 4,000,000 farms was valued at a little over $12 billion, and equipment and machinery at $407 million; by 1900 there were 5,737,000 farms valued at nearly $20.5 billion, with equipment and machinery worth $750 million; the more than 6,000,000 farms of 1910 were worth double the 1900 figure. The growth of agriculture was aided by the appearance of newly invented or improved farm machinery, for it was at this time that American agriculture was thoroughly mechanized. The reaper and the thresher were in use before the Civil War and were followed in later years by the disc harrow, the gang plow, cottonseed planters, the giant combine harvester-thresher, the cream separator, commercially produced fertilizer, and, in the early twentieth century, the gas engine tractor. Although farmers had bad years and sometimes were paid very low prices for their major crops such as wheat and corn, there were other years in which they prospered. The domestic demand grew and export sales boomed when war or bad weather caused European nations to buy American grain on a large scale.

The road to economic growth was not without its potholes. Three severe depressions, brought on in large part by the Robber Barons and their followers, occurred in 1873, 1893, and 1907. The first one was a direct result of overbuilding of railroads, overexpansion of agriculture, and a great deal of speculation in the stock markets. The 1873 depression was triggered by the collapse in September of the prestigious investment banking house of Jay Cooke. The depression lingered for six years, with as many as three million unemployed, little railroad building, a sharp drop in prices, and a decrease in immigration. The depression finally eased, aided by a boom in agriculture, which increased railroad traffic, when good crops in America coincided with a period of poor crops in Europe.

The depression that began in 1893 followed much the same pattern and stemmed from much the same causes. Agriculture had been in a depressed condition for several years and railroad expansion had again gone too far too fast. A financial panic began when a large London investment house collapsed and European interests withdrew capital from the United States. Many railroads went into bankruptcy and banks failed—about 600 of them by the end of 1893. The number of persons out of work rose to 2,500,000. Good times gradually returned by 1897 when America sold Europe almost twice as much grain as in the previous year. Europe also bought more American manufactured articles, while at home the neglected railroads required repairs and equipment.

The bad times of 1907 were more in the nature of a financial panic and did not result in a prolonged depression. Overspeculation in the financial centers of the nation brought on the trouble, with the inadequately regulated trust companies largely at fault.

On the whole, the nation prospered greatly from 1865 to 1913, but many people came to think the price being paid was too high. The conscience of the nation, increasingly uncomfortable, began to call for placing some restraints on the Robber Barons and their henchmen.

3
The Spirit of the Nation, 1865–1913

Before the Civil War, American business and industry, for the most part, existed as local and comparatively small units. No one merchant or manufacturer could exercise full control over the prices he charged his customers for goods or the service he rendered. Even the wage earner had some bargaining power with his employer, or could leave one small firm for another—or, at one extreme, move west "to grow up with the country." After the war, industrial units not only became larger and therefore more powerful in relation to customers and employees, but also became fewer. Such a situation made it easier for supposedly competing firms to join in fixing prices and dividing markets, and more difficult for customers and workers, as small, weak individual economic units, to exercise much choice of product or job.

The growing disparity in economic strength became evident as the railroad network spread, both because the roads were the first big industries and because, in early railroading days in many places, one road had a monopoly. Before long, railroads began to abuse their position, but it was some time before protests became widespread and organized. For one thing, most Americans, even those with little material wealth, did not question the rightness of the principle of individual enterprise, free from governmental intervention or regulation. Even before the middle of the nineteenth century, this point of view had become accepted as the American way. Under the changed circumstances of economic life in the second half of the century, however, more and more people turned to state and federal governments for protection against monopolistic practices.

The railroads were the first to feel the results of this change in attitude, beginning with attempts by some state governments to control freight rates, at least within their borders. The drive for such laws was spearheaded by the National Grange of Patrons of Husbandry, founded in 1867 and reaching its peak membership of 858,000 in 1875. Its main target, besides the roads, were the grain storage elevators, often owned by the roads, which were likewise accused of charging unfairly high rates for their use. In addition, many farmers and small town merchants were bitter because they had bought railroad bonds or voted for their community to buy them in order to have access to transportation, only to find that the roads then turned around and gouged them for the service.

The result was the passage of a series of so-called Granger laws, beginning with legislation in Illinois in 1871 and 1873. Iowa and Wisconsin enacted similar laws in 1874, and by the early 1880's Nebraska, Kansas and Missouri moved to control railroads by legislation. In those days, too, the farmers and merchants were supported by the Supreme Court. In 1876 the court, in the case of *Munn* v. *Illinois,* upheld a law that set maximum rates for grain storage. The court also decided that states could fix maximum freight and passenger rates, not only within the state but elsewhere so long as there was no national legislation by Congress. The court, however, reversed itself in 1886 in the *Wabash* case, involving another Illinois law, and ruled that states could not regulate rates on shipments that went outside their borders.

At this same time the report of a Senate committee, headed by Shelby M. Cullom, documented the shoddy practices of the railroads and recommended the creation of a national commission to regulate the roads. The movement to curb the railroads culminated in the passage of the Interstate Commerce Act of 1887 which created a five-man commission. The railroads were required to charge "reasonable and just rates," and were forbidden to give rebates or to charge more for a short haul than a long haul. The Commission could not itself set rates and any decision it made could be challenged in the courts. The railroads used this procedure to delay the enforcement of commission orders. The commission received some support from the Supreme Court in 1896 when the justices agreed that railroads could be forced to testify, but almost all the cases involving rates were decided in favor of the railroads—fifteen out of sixteen between 1887 and 1905.

The Elkins Act of 1903 was a further attempt to crack down on the rebate system. A still stronger law was the Hepburn Act of 1906, which gave the Commission the power to set "just and reasonable" maximum rates and gave it authority over other common carriers, such as pipelines. A final step in this period was the passage of the Mann-Elkins Act in 1910, which extended the Commission's jurisdiction to telephone, telegraph, and cable companies. It also authorized the Commission to suspend proposed new rates until a railroad could prove their reasonableness. As slow as these laws were in achieving the results hoped for by their supporters, the Interstate Commerce Act was a notable milestone because it established the principle of federal regulation in cases where the public interest required it and where the separate states could not cope with the situation.

The growing agitation for protection against the alleged evils of the trusts and the monopolies resulted in the passage by Congress in 1890 of the Sherman Antitrust Act, which declared: "Every contract, combination in the form of trust or otherwise, or conspiracy, in restraint of trade or commerce among the several states, or with foreign nations, is hereby declared to be illegal. . . ." To the layman, this seemed clear enough, but to judges the language was vague enough so that it could be interpreted much as one wished. For the first ten years, the federal government, controlled mostly by men friendly to big business, brought only eighteen court actions. The most important of the early cases was decided by the Supreme Court in favor of big business. In 1895 it declared that the Sugar Trust, which controlled the manufacture of almost all the sugar in the country, was not engaged in interstate commerce because manufacturing was not interstate commerce. The court also was able to find that operating a railroad was not interstate commerce and therefore the Sherman Act did not apply to the lines. The court did, however, have no difficulty in applying this act to labor unions, deciding that certain of their actions were "in restraint of trade." On the whole the Sherman Act was a disappointment to farmers, laborers, and reformers in general. In 1914, during President Wilson's administration, the Clayton Antitrust Act became law and it contained provisions intended to stop up the holes in the Sherman Act. It forbade practices which "substantially tended" to lessen competition, such as price-fixing; labor unions and agricultural cooperatives were declared not subject to the law; and the use of injunctions against labor was restricted. Once again, however, the courts came to the rescue of big business and interpreted the new law so as to render it nearly meaningless.

Spurred by Upton Sinclair's novel revealing the disgusting conditions under which meat was packed, and with the energetic support of President Roosevelt, a meat inspection law was passed in 1906. At the same time, stimulated by magazine exposés of patent medicines and a campaign by Dr. Harvey W. Wiley, chief chemist of the Department of Agriculture, against the preservatives and adulterants being used in canned foods, a Pure Food and Drug Act became law. Both laws helped improve the situation, but they required strengthening in later years.

The dissatisfaction—sometimes amounting to rage—felt by many against the new men of wealth and their octopuslike industries was expressed politically, first through the Populist movement and a little later through the Progressives. The Populist movement began in the 1880's with the formation of a number of Farmers' Alliances in the agricultural states of the South and West. In 1890 candidates representing the point of view of the movement won fourteen seats in the House of Representatives. Two years later a formal national organization came into being, named the People's party, although usually called Populist. In a national convention the party nominated its own candidate for president, James B. Weaver (1833–1912), a longtime crusader for reform and a brigade commander in the Civil War.

More important than the candidate was the Populist platform. It called for the unlimited coinage of silver in the belief that this would make money cheaper and aid farmers with large mortgages and other debtors; control of the currency system by the government rather than the banks; public ownership of the railroads and the telephone and telegraph systems; restriction of immigration; the eight-hour day for labor; the secret ballot; and the direct election of senators by the people instead of by state legislatures. The legislatures were suspected of being open to bribery by business interests. The party also proposed a complicated credit system for farmers, based on their crops, that would, it was hoped, free them from domination by the banks. The Populists carried four states with twenty-two electoral votes in 1892, the first time since 1860 that a third party had won any such votes, and they elected ten congressmen and five senators. The Democrats, however, won the White House and both houses of Congress.

In 1896 the Populists joined the Democrats in supporting William Jennings Bryan, but while Bryan received strong support from farmers, he was unable to sway the majority of the working men of the East. This marked the end of the Populist movement for practical purposes, but its spirit and some of its ideas lived on in the Progressives and even later in the days of the New Deal in the 1930's. The Populists were, however, basically old-fashioned, and whether knowingly or not were trying to turn the clock back to a simpler, rural America.

The Progressives of the early twentieth century, on the other hand, were urban oriented and primarily concerned with the problems of the new industrialism, corruption in government, and the assimilation of immigrants into American culture. The Progressives were led by urban, middle-class Protestants whose actions implied that they were best fitted to rule and to bring about reform. While they feared the large corporations and wanted to break them up, they feared labor unions almost as much. Working through both major parties, the Progressives secured legislation intended to reform business, and they agitated for corporation and personal income taxes. At the time there was a good deal of corruption in municipal government in many states and the Progressives made a major contribution in ending some of this and in installing mayors who were honest and efficient administrators.

In the early years of the century, the Progressives looked to

Theodore Roosevelt for leadership after this dynamic and versatile man became president in 1901, when President William McKinley was assassinated. He won the office in his own right in the election of 1904, although many Republicans supported him somewhat reluctantly because of his growing reputation as an enemy of big business. In his first term he called for more regulation of corporations, but Congress did not support him. Roosevelt attacked what he called "the malefactors of great wealth," and supported such measures as the Hepburn Act, but many of his Progressive supporters thought his administration did not exert itself enough to enforce the Sherman Antitrust Act. Roosevelt, on his part, spoke of "trust busting," and forty suits were begun in his administration against such organizations. He was also the first president to push for practical action to conserve the nation's resources and he added 150 million acres of public land to the government reserves.

It was Roosevelt, too, who in 1906 coined the term "Muckrakers" to describe the journalists who in magazine articles and books exposed government corruption and the evils of the trusts. He did not intend to use the word to praise these writers, but the Progressives hailed their work and used it as ammunition in securing legislation aimed at controlling civic corruption and corporate power. Among the influential books that attacked big business were Ida M. Tarbell's *History of the Standard Oil Company,* which began as a series of magazine articles in 1902. Ray Stannard Baker's *Railroads on Trial;* and Thomas W. Lawson's *Frenzied Finance. Wealth Against Commonwealth,* by Henry Demarest Lloyd, attacked concentrated wealth and monopolies, while John Moody, in *Truth about the Trusts,* found that by 1904, 318 great industrial corporations existed, that nearly three-fourths of them were formed in the previous six years, and that more than half of them were large enough to control prices and production in their industries. Outstanding among exposés of governmental corruption was Lincoln Steffens' *Shame of the Cities.* Several novelists besides Sinclair used fiction in the crusade, one example being Frank Norris's *The Octopus,* the story of farmers fighting the domination of the Southern Pacific Railroad.

In 1873 there appeared a novel, *The Gilded Age,* written

jointly by Mark Twain, the popular humorist, and C. D. Warner, which gave its name to most of the period under discussion. The novel's plot and subplots satirize the greed, speculation, and corruption of the times, and the characters include a thinly disguised senator and a well-known stock market speculator, among others. In some accounts, the Gilded Age is considered to have begun at the end of the Civil War, but a more appropriate beginning might be the start of Ulysses S. Grant's first term as president in early 1869. Sometimes the Gilded Age is considered to have ended about 1890, but in light of the events of the time, the term can well be used to cover the years to the turn of the century, when the Progressive era gradually took over. In any event, it was a period of greed, corruption, and vulgarity in business, politics, and society.

The trusts and the monopolies reached the peak of their power in these years. Newly rich families showed off their wealth by building mansions costing a million dollars or more. These showy homes were but one visible aspect of the growing gap between those at the top and the very poor, mostly recent immigrants, who lived in slums as new as the mansions. Legislators invited bribes and some senators acted as though they represented a particular economic interest rather than the people of their states. The spirit of the age did include a strong feeling of optimism and of confidence in the future. This encouraged ambitious men, whether in politics or industry, to act only in their own self-interest, to feel that the ends justified the means, and that to the victor belonged all the spoils he could seize. It seems fitting, then, that Machinery Hall, which featured a very large steam engine with a thirty-foot flywheel, was the premier attraction of the Centennial Exposition, held in Philadelphia in 1876 to celebrate the first hundred years of independence.

Out of the economic, political, and social atmosphere of the Gilded Age marched the small group of men who became known as the Robber Barons—and who, incidentally, were closely followed by thousands of other men who would have been large-scale Robber Barons, too, if they had been clever or lucky enough. The Robber Barons were products of their times. The spirit of free enterprise and a benevolent attitude by government encouraged them to do what was of the most benefit to them, not to the country. Natural resources and new technologies were means to their ends and were waiting to be used by those who first recognized the possibilities. At the same time, these men were individuals, differing in some ways in their backgrounds, abilities, methods, and goals. Let us take a closer look at some of these unusual men.

4

How to Milk a Railroad

Among the first of the Robber Barons were four men—Cornelius Vanderbilt, Daniel Drew, James Fisk, Jr., and Jay Gould—who were never surpassed in their devotion to making money by any means available and with utter disregard for the good of the public or the nation. The public was especially unfortunate in relation to these four because they chose some of the country's most important railroads as the focus of their greed. To them (Vanderbilt being an exception to some extent), railroads were not freight and passenger carriers vital to the development of the nation; rather, they were corporate organizations whose stocks and bonds could be manipulated so as to pour forth a stream of money.

The oldest, and first of the four to accumulate a fortune, was Cornelius Vanderbilt (1794–1877). He was, in fact, the first American after John Jacob Astor (1763–1848) to amass a fortune large enough to stand comparison with the wealth of almost anyone who followed. Born on Staten Island, New York, on May 27, 1794, Vanderbilt was the son of a farmer of Dutch descent and a mother of English descent. About a month before his seventeenth birthday, his mother agreed to lend him one hundred dollars to buy a boat if he would plow and plant an eight-acre field. Cornelius did so and set himself up to ferry goods and passengers between Manhattan and Staten islands. Before long, the ener-

getic young boatman was operating three ferries. He prospered
further during the War of 1812 by winning a contract to keep
military posts in the New York harbor area supplied.

Vanderbilt was among the astute young men of the shipping
business who saw that steamships were rapidly replacing sailing
vessels and so he resolved to get into that field. Accordingly, in
1818 he undertook to operate the steamships of a man who owned
several and in that way he learned the business and saved money.
By 1829 he went into steam shipping for himself with a steamer
built to his own design. Vanderbilt operated a freight and
passenger service on the Hudson River, first as far north as
Putnam County, then to Albany. On this route he ran into
competition from another of these four early promoters, Daniel
Drew. They engaged in a rate war in which passenger fares were
slashed to almost nothing. When, however, Vanderbilt bought
out Drew, rates were restored to their earlier and higher levels.
In 1834 Vanderbilt accepted $100,000 from a rival shipping group
to withdraw from the Hudson. He then turned his attention to
Long Island Sound where he began operating a steamship line
that went to Providence, Rhode Island. By the 1840's Vanderbilt
was operating more steamships than anyone else in the nation,
and was already known as Commodore Vanderbilt, a title that
remained with him long after he abandoned shipping for railroading.

Moving with the times, the Commodore entered the transatlantic shipping arena, where there was a great deal of competition. He first operated two ships in 1855, with Le Havre, France,
as the European destination. He lost money at the start, but
answered that challenge by building a larger passenger liner
which sailed to Southampton, England, as well as Le Havre. Vanderbilt became the leading American figure in transatlantic
shipping until the Civil War, when many American ships were
taken over by the government.

The discovery of gold in California in 1849 created a demand
for steamship facilities to transport fortune hunters from the East
coast to either the Isthmus of Panama or Nicaragua and for other
ships in the Pacific to carry them on north to San Francisco. The
land barriers were crossed by pack mules on roads hacked out of
the jungle and by boats on lakes and rivers. Vanderbilt was not

one to miss such an opportunity and by 1851 he and some associates were operating ships on both oceans. They also had a charter giving them the exclusive right to cross Nicaragua by boat and carriage. The company, in addition, made plans, never carried out, for building a canal to link the oceans. The Commodore retired—temporarily as it turned out—from this Central American operation in late 1852 and the next year took his family and a large party to Europe on his yacht. By then the one-time farm boy with almost no education was worth about $11 million, which he estimated was invested so as to bring him a return of 25 percent each year. By 1860 this fortune had increased to $20 million.

When the Civil War broke out in 1861, Vanderbilt was a strong supporter of the Union and offered his steamer *Vanderbilt* to the government. The offer was accepted and although the Commodore apparently meant to lend it only for the duration, the government thanked him profusely and kept the ship. In late 1862, Vanderbilt undertook to outfit a number of ships to carry troops from the East Coast to New Orleans. He did not ask any compensation, but when it was discovered that some of the ships were so unseaworthy that they could not make the trip, Vanderbilt narrowly avoided a Congressional vote of censure.

Steamships had hardly begun to replace sailing ships before the building of railroads brought new competition in the transportation field. At first the Commodore did not think much of the possibilities of the steam locomotive, perhaps because he was badly injured in 1833 the first time he ever took a train trip. Before long, however, his sharp judgment as to where money could be made drew him into the railroad field and, eventually, away from shipping. He became a director of the Long Island Railroad in 1845, but held the position for less than two years. Also in 1845 he bought stock in the Providence and Stonington Railroad. The base of the vast fortune Vanderbilt accumulated through his railroad ventures was laid, however, in the 1850's when he bought stocks and bonds of the New York and Harlem Railroad. His first connection with the Erie Railroad, which was to lead him into one of the most distressing financial adventures of his career, began in 1854 and he became a director in 1859.

The Harlem route ran north from New York, inland from the

Hudson River, while the Hudson River Railroad followed the east bank. Vanderbilt's interest in the Harlem grew until he controlled it, and by 1863, with the aid of some tricky dealings in the stock market, he also acquired control of the Hudson. The next step was to purchase enough stock to gain control of the New York Central Railroad, which ran across New York State from Albany to Buffalo. The final step in the expansion of the first Vanderbilt railroad empire was the merging of these three lines in 1869. Under the Commodore's direction it was a well-run road, a matter of pride with him, no matter how much he might manipulate stocks in order to make a few more millions. In the course of acquiring the three lines, Vanderbilt and his colleagues issued nearly $50 million of new stock and he, as befitted the leader, received about half of these securities at no cost.

Sometimes Vanderbilt's partner in schemes to manipulate the stock market, sometimes Vanderbilt's devious enemy, Daniel Drew (1797–1879) also made a great deal of money but was not as clever as Vanderbilt when it came to holding on to it. Drew was another farm boy, born at Carmel, New York, who, as he wrote, "reached the age of fifteen without much book-learning." Although underage at the time of the War of 1812, he enlisted for the sake of a one hundred dollar bounty and served for three months, at which point the war ended.

Drew used his bounty money to become a drover, buying livestock and driving it to market in the city. He abandoned this for a short while to travel with a circus, but only until he had saved more money to expand his cattle business. When he took a herd to the city, he fed the cattle salt to make them thirsty; then, shortly before they were to be sold by the pound, he let them drink all the water they wanted, thus adding to their weight and hence to the amount he got for them. The watering of livestock provided a common term for Wall Street, "watered stock" meaning that issued so as to raise the capitalization of a company without putting any new assets behind the stock. Drew was also the first person to drive livestock to the New York market from Ohio.

After selling his first Hudson River boat to Vanderbilt, Drew later went into another Hudson River shipping venture with a group of men. But he also formed another company of his own which operated under still another man's name. Drew then got himself appointed by the first company to try to buy out the other, which he did at a price $8,000 higher than originally intended, all of which went into his pocket. Drew was sorry to see the Civil War end, he admitted, because in 1862 alone, "Abe Lincoln paid me $350,000" for the use of his boats.

Drew also became a broker on Wall Street, where, he said, he was too busy making money to care about such problems as slavery. In the stock market, he declared, "The dog that snaps the quickest gets the bone." He bragged of the trick he played on another operator when he "accidentally" let him see what seemed to be orders to buy large quantities of Erie Railroad stock. Since he was presumed to have inside information, the story was spread quickly and others began buying. Drew, as intended all along, actually sold Erie stock at the prevailing high price, which did not continue for long.

Since railroads were the most rapidly expanding industries of the time, just about every financier and speculator became involved in dealing in their stocks, and Drew was no exception. His first such venture was to join with Vanderbilt to buy control of the Boston and Stonington Railroad, a New England line. Drew's attention soon turned to the Erie Railroad, as did that of almost every investor and speculator in rails, for in the 1850's and later, the Erie was one of the biggest businesses in the country. During the panic of 1857, Drew set out to get control, a formidable task for one man. When the road ran short of money and when Drew, a director, sowed seeds of dissension among his fellow directors, he offered to come to the rescue by lending the Erie $1.5 million.

Using his inside position, he "speckilated" (he always spelled it that way) and was able to make the price of the stock rise and fall almost as he wished. One of his tricks was to get a crony to apply for an injunction forbidding the road to pay dividends because of its large debt. The stock went down, and Drew bought; then he had the request withdrawn, the stock went up and Drew sold. He got a dose of his own medicine, though, when he tried to outsmart Vanderbilt in manipulating the stock of the Harlem Railroad. Drew sold a large number of shares "short"—that is, he sold stock he didn't own, gambling that the price would go down and that he could buy at a lower price the shares he needed to make good his sales by the time he had to deliver them. Unfortunately for Drew,

more shares were sold short than existed. He had to beg
Vanderbilt, to whom he owed the shares, to let him off, but the
Commodore would do nothing for his "old friend" and the
incident cost Drew at least half a million dollars. It may have been
at that time that he composed the rhyme attributed to him: "He
that sells what isn't his'n, / Must buy it back, or go to prison."

None of the speculators of the time contrasted more with
grim, dour Daniel Drew than jolly, outgoing James Fisk, Jr.
(1834–72), who learned some of the tricks of Wall Street from
Drew. Fisk was born in Pownal, Vermont, on April 1, 1834, and
spent his boyhood in Brattleboro, Vermont. His Yankee father
was a traveling peddler and Fisk helped him for a while, but when
he was fifteen he ran away with a circus. Back home when he was
eighteen, he took up peddling for himself. By the time he was
twenty-one Fisk had five wagons on the road, all of them brightly
painted like circus wagons, very catching to the eye.

Offered a job in Boston by a large merchandiser there, Fisk
moved there in 1860 to become a wholesale salesman, but
surprisingly, and to his embarrassment, he was a failure. When
the Civil War started, Fisk persuaded his employers to send him
to Washington where he entertained generals and members of
Congress on a lavish scale. He became one of the first war
profiteers when he sold the government several thousand blan-
kets that proved to be mildewed. Fisk turned his attention to
bootlegging cotton out of the South, a profitable but illegal
business. His first deal was in 1862, and on one of his trips he was
nearly captured by Confederate troops. Later he went to New
Orleans where he is said to have bought as much as $800,000
worth of cotton in a single day. As the war neared its end, Fisk
thought up a scheme to make money in London by selling
Confederate bonds short. With others supplying the capital, he
arranged for a steamer to receive word by telegraph in Halifax,
Nova Scotia, of the South's surrender and then sailed for England
as fast as possible. The scheme worked and Fisk's agent had two
days in London in which to sell $5 million of bonds before anyone
else heard the news that caused the bonds' value to collapse
entirely.

Fisk was ready in late 1864 to invade Wall Street, but he was overconfident and soon lost in the stock market all he had made on the Confederate bond scheme. Borrowing money in Boston, he returned to the fray in late 1865 and became an ally of Drew. That shrewd dealer was pleased with his protégé when he sold at a high price nine steamers Drew owned. The next year Fisk profited handsomely from one of Drew's coups with Erie stock. As collateral for a loan to the railroad (of which he was now treasurer) Drew took fifty-eight thousand shares. Outsiders did not know he had them, and Drew, secretly using Fisk as one of his brokers, began selling these shares while the price was high. The large number of shares drove the stock down, whereupon Drew bought back the shares at a much lower price. He was happy to know that Vanderbilt was one of the big losers.

The youngest of the four despoilers of railroads was Jay Gould (1836–92), who was Vanderbilt's successor when it came to manipulating railroad stocks and piling up money. Gould was also a farm boy and was born in Delaware County, New York, on May 27, 1836. He disliked farm life intensely and quit school at fourteen because he wanted to make money. While clerking long hours in a store, he taught himself surveying at night and found a job as an assistant surveyor at twenty dollars a month. A by-product of this work was a history of Delaware County which he wrote in 1856 when he was only twenty.

That same year the ambitious Gould formed a partnership with seventy-year-old Zadoc Pratt to operate a tannery in Lehigh County, Pennsylvania. Pratt was to be put in most of the money, although Gould had already saved up five thousand dollars, and Gould was to operate the plant. In less than a year, Pratt discovered that Gould had used a good deal of the tannery's income to start a private bank in a nearby town, but instead of pressing charges, Pratt let Gould buy him out. To be able to do this, the latter had to find a partner with sufficient capital and did so by interesting Charles M. Leupp, one of New York City's most prosperous leather merchants, in the proposition. This time Gould used the firm's money to speculate in the leather market and he attempted to corner it—that is, to buy so many hides that those who had sold him hides short would be unable to make good on their promises. Just then, however, the Panic of 1857 struck and Gould was on the verge of bankruptcy. At this point Leupp found out that Gould had been using both his money and his name to finance his speculation and committed suicide.

Leupp's brother-in-law, David W. Lee, tried to salvage something from the financial ruins and also to punish Gould. Gould attempted to operate the tannery as though Lee had no rights in it, whereupon the latter decided on direct action. He went to Scranton in March 1860 and hired a gang of unemployed miners and town toughs to seize the tannery by force, which they did. Not to be outdone, Gould also organized an armed force which, outnumbering its opponents, attacked the tannery. Gould's forces won, wounding or beating up all the defenders.

This disorder and several court actions caused Gould to close the tannery and move to New York where he set up as a leather merchant, although he was already more interested in railroads. Three years before he had used some of the tannery funds to buy into the Washington and Rutland Railroad. Now, with his father-in-law's aid, he secured a controlling interest and became president of the railroad at the age of twenty-seven. He proved an excellent manager but soon sold out—at a substantial profit. In the meantime, Gould became a partner in a Wall Street broker-age firm and, as the Civil War began, saw that it would provide many opportunities of which a sharp mind could take advantage. He had no intention of enlisting or of being drafted, and he avoided military service by paying for a substitute. Around the time the war ended in 1865, Gould showed interest in the Erie Railroad and became acquainted with Drew and Fisk. He bought enough shares so that by 1867 he was elected a director.

The careers of these four men—Vanderbilt, Drew, Fisk, and Gould—came together in one of the most outrageous incidents in American business history—the milking of the Erie Railroad of millions of dollars. When the Erie was completed in 1851, running from Piermont, on the west side of the Hudson near New York City, to Dunkirk on Lake Erie, it was 483 miles long, the longest railroad in the world at the time. By 1868 it had added branch lines that brought its mileage to 773, and it required fifteen thousand employees to operate it. Newer roads gave the Erie connections to the west, while the oil traffic, growing since the discovery of petroleum in Pennsylvania in 1859, was bringing it new business.

Nevertheless, with Drew in control in recent years, the tracks and the rolling stock had been badly neglected in favor of manipulation and speculation in Erie stock and bonds. At the same time, Vanderbilt was scheming to get control because the Erie was the chief competitor of his New York Central Railroad for traffic from New York westward. The contest began in 1867 with Drew, assisted by the two younger men, Fisk and Gould, as one party, a group of Boston financiers as a second, and the Commodore a third. Vanderbilt and the Boston men first agreed to gang up on Drew and oust him as a director, but when Vanderbilt broke this agreement, the Bostonians joined Drew's side. Vanderbilt resorted to legal tactics, getting a judge who almost certainly was bribed, to prevent Drew from using the shares of stock he had on hand. Meanwhile, the Commodore was buying large numbers of shares. The opposing trio decided to make available to him all the stock they could. They had the Erie directors authorize them to issue $10 million of convertible bonds, which they quickly changed to 100,000 shares of stock, which they dumped on the market in spite of a court injunction Vanderbilt had secured from the same helpful judge. The trio kept a printing press in the basement of Erie headquarters just for printing stock and by March 10, 1868, $8 million worth had been bought by the Commodore. At this point he knew he was beaten and he still did not have control of the Erie.

The next day Drew, Fisk, and Gould were about to divide the spoils when they heard that Vanderbilt's friendly judge had issued a contempt of court citation against them. Hastily they crammed $4 million, the part of the money they had on hand in paper currency, into a bag and fled by boat to Jersey City, New Jersey, on the other side of the Hudson. Here they took over Taylor's Hotel, which was soon dubbed Fort Taylor because, with Fisk as commander, the trio engaged a band of armed guards to protect them. Fisk, tongue in cheek, announced that since Vanderbilt controlled New York, they had decided to move west "to grow up with the country." While Vanderbilt got a New York judge to declare the Erie in receivership, Gould transferred the legal incorporation of the road from New York to New Jersey.

Although safe as long as they stayed in New Jersey, the Erie gang realized that Vanderbilt was busy influencing New York judges and the state legislature. Accordingly, Gould packed his clothes and $500,000 in cash and set out for the state capital, Albany, in spite of the danger of arrest. He had hardly arrived when he was arrested by order of a Vanderbilt judge, but was released on $500,000 bail. Gould then set about bribing the legislators, which was not difficult. His opponent in the bribery contest, representing Vanderbilt, was William Marcy ("Boss") Tweed (1823–78), of Tammany Hall, whose Tweed Ring was busy at the time fleecing the city of New York, whose politics it controlled, of millions of dollars. Tweed later said he handed out $180,000 in bribes, while Gould was at least as generous. At first the Assembly voted down Gould's bill, which would have authorized the Erie directors to issue as much stock as they wished, but the Senate approved it. Vanderbilt then gave up the struggle, so the Assembly changed its mind, since no more bribes were to be had from that source, and passed the bill.

During this time, Drew was unhappy in Jersey City and longed for a solution to the struggle so that he could get back to New York. When Vanderbilt had a message smuggled to him that he, too, was tired of the fight, Drew slipped away to the city on a Sunday when a civil summons could not be served. Fisk and Gould learned of these dealings behind their backs and also that Drew had taken the Erie's cash with him. He had, however, left his personal funds in New Jersey, and Fisk lost no time in getting a judge to attach them. The pair decided they would have to come to terms, too, or everyone would combine against them and squeeze them out. After several days of argument, it was agreed that Vanderbilt would receive $4.75 million for half the shares that had flowed so freely from the printing press and that the balance would be paid for within six months. The Boston group got $4 million for some practically worthless bonds of another railroad. Drew was made to contribute $540,000 of his profits toward the deal, while Fisk and Gould ended up with no profit but with control of the Erie. Accordingly, Gould became president on July 2, 1868, and Fisk comptroller and managing director. They also had the satisfaction of forcing Drew to sever all connection with the road. Boss Tweed, formerly the Commodore's ally, was welcomed as a director, largely because at least three judges would do whatever he told them to do.

Gould and Fisk celebrated by issuing $20 million worth of stock between July and October, most of the proceeds going into their pockets. They also used the stock to trap Drew through a stock market manipulation. The Erie now entered a long period in which it paid no dividends, and money from stock and bond sales went into the pockets of insiders instead of improving the run-down physical facilities. The latest in a series of serious accidents on the road occurred on July 14, 1869, when nine persons were burned to death and ten more injured.

For Gould and Fisk, though, the year 1869 was notable for a bloody struggle, with slapstick overtones, for control of a small railroad called the Albany and Susquehanna. This road ran from Albany, New York, to a junction with the Erie at Binghamton, New York. If the pair could secure control, they could give Vanderbilt's New York Central more competition because the Albany and Susquehanna would furnish the Erie a connection with New England through Albany. Completed only in January 1869, by June the road was a target of the Erie rulers. The quest for enough stock to gain or hold control was a complicated one, with one faction of the directors favoring Gould and Fisk, the other strongly opposed. Both sides used the judiciary to get contrary orders and rulings. At that time New York State voters elected judges by districts, but all were equal, so that a judge in one area could undo what another did elsewhere.

In Albany, where a directors' meeting was to be held, Fisk and his bodyguard were forcibly prevented from entering the session. Each side continued to hurl judges' orders at the other, so Fisk decided to try a new tactic. He wired the Erie superintendent at Binghamton to gather a force, seize the Albany and Susquehanna terminal there, and start a train northward. The opposition in Albany had the same idea and started a train south, manning it with a lawyer and nearly a hundred husky railroad workers. Each side served the orders of its friendly judges on the railroad station personnel along the way. On August 10, the two trains were approaching each other about fifteen miles east of Binghamton. To the south was the Fisk-Gould force that eventually numbered about 800, to the north the smaller Albany and Susquehanna force of about 400. The trains halted at opposite ends of a 2,200-foot tunnel and remained there for some hours. Meanwhile, the mayor of Binghamton wired the governor in Albany to send the militia.

Toward evening the Erie train started through the tunnel and discovered, when it emerged, that the Albany and Susquehanna train was headed toward it. The Erie engineer was the first to put on his brakes but the two locomotives collided head on. The warriors of the two sides jumped off the trains and a hand-to-hand battle followed. The Erie forces fled but rallied at the entrance of the tunnel where their reserves were stationed. Both sides eventually backed off with a good many broken limbs, bruises, and bloody noses, but with only two bullet wounds, both suffered by Erie supporters. By now the state militia was on the scene and the war was over. Back in Albany, both sides played more legal games until in February the anti-Erie management leased the Albany and Susquehanna in perpetuity to the Delaware and Hudson Canal Company, a powerful organization with which Gould and Fisk decided not to wage war. Fisk, who could laugh at his own misfortunes, said of the affair, "Nothing is lost save honor." Charles Francis Adams, however, saw it as "armed warfare between corporations."

Three of the four men who had ruined the Erie Railroad for their personal gain were now ready to move on to other, if not better, enterprises.

5

After Erie: Vanderbilt, Drew, Fisk, and Gould

When the Erie wars were over, Vanderbilt was in his seventies but was by no means ready to retire. Drew was not much younger, was ruined financially, and never regained the position he had once held. Fisk and Gould, being younger, could look forward to new worlds to plunder, which Gould did on a continental scale, but Fisk, a victim of his own exuberant nature, met a bloody end after a few turbulent years.

Vanderbilt put together a through route from New York to Chicago by linking his New York Central to the Lake Shore and Michigan Southern, which he bought. He recapitalized his whole system in 1869 at $86 million, which almost doubled the book value, and which meant that a great deal of it was watered stock. In spite of this, Vanderbilt's railroad made money and paid regular dividends. One reason was that the Commodore, in spite of his financial tactics, saw to it that the roads were improved with steel rails and bridges, kept in good repair, and efficiently managed. The route from Albany to Buffalo, already double-tracked, had two more tracks added in 1873 and 1874, and between 1869 and 1871 he built a large new station, Grand Central Depot, on Forty-second Street in New York. The structure was 249 feet wide and 695 feet long from north to south, a very imposing building at that time.

Like all railroad men of the time, Vanderbilt was often involved in rate wars with rival lines. In a contest with the Erie in 1870, he lowered the rate on shipping cattle from Buffalo to New York to one dollar for a whole carload. Jim Fisk, who enjoyed a little fun along with business, thereupon quietly bought up six thousand head of cattle and shipped them on his rival's road, making a good profit on the deal. Vanderbilt entered into several "gentlemen's agreements" with other roads, which were intended to eliminate cutthroat competition, but these agreements seldom lasted for long. At one time a passenger could travel from New York to Chicago for five dollars, whereas in the summer of 1876 wheat was carried over the same route for only ten cents a bushel.

Cornelius Vanderbilt died on January 4, 1877, leaving a fortune of about $100 million, almost all of which went to his son William Henry. Vanderbilt thought of himself as a plain, blunt man, which he was. Perhaps his family background and slight education made him seem rougher than he really was, but those who competed with him considered him completely ruthless. He certainly was unscrupulous and selfish, but he was also an unusually capable man. Once he acquired a property and decided to keep it, he worked just as hard at improving it as he did at squeezing every penny possible out of it. The Commodore never had any social ambitions, but he was an enthusiastic horseman and took great pride in owning the best and fastest horses he could find. His only notable contribution out of his fortune to a worthy cause was the $1 million he gave between 1873 and his death to Central University, a Methodist institution in Nashville, Tennessee, which was renamed for him. In his later years Vanderbilt turned more and more to spiritualism, in which he had shown an interest for some time. In séances he attempted to get information about the future trend of the stock market and once even tried to contact the spirit of Jim Fisk for a helpful look into the future. Although he probably never really said it, Vanderbilt's attitude toward business and the public is summed up in the words attributed to him: "Law! What do I care about law? Hain't I got the power?"

Vanderbilt had nine daughters and three sons, and of the latter, George was the Commodore's favorite. However, George contracted a serious illness while serving in the Civil War and died soon after. The oldest son, William Henry Vanderbilt (1821–85), did not stand high in his father's opinion for many years. His father bought William a farm on Staten Island and, against his expectations, the son made a success of it. After he had also shown his competence in managing a railroad on Staten Island, William moved to New York when he was forty-three to run the Harlem line. After his father's death, William became head of the family's various properties. He was not the ruthless battler his father had been, but he got along moderately well in the cutthroat world of railroad competition. Even if he was not a fighter, William Vanderbilt's attitude toward the world was much the same as his father's. He once remarked: "The public be damned," an opinion held by all the Robber Barons, judging by their actions.

Daniel Drew's business career, unlike Vanderbilt's, ended unhappily for him. Early in 1868 he bragged that he was worth $13 million and that "all my eggs had two yolks." By autumn he was ousted from the Erie but ready for one more fling in its stock. In full control of the Erie, Gould and Fisk were issuing new stock regularly, claiming it was needed to make improvements on the road. As they sold these large quantities, Erie stock went down in price. Drew joined his former comrades in selling Erie short but continued to do so after Gould and Fisk stopped. This gave them a chance to punish the old trader for what they felt had been his treacherous moves in going secretly to Vanderbilt at the height of the fight for control of the Erie Railroad. They turned around and began buying Erie stock, using some of the $12 million they had collected from the sale of new stock and which they had held out of circulation. The price of Erie stock began to go up and Drew was caught owing some forty thousand shares he did not have. Even though he threatened various legal actions against Gould and Fisk, the pair showed no mercy and refused to let him have any of their shares. In the end, Drew lost about $1.5 million, but Gould and Fisk came out of the affray without much profit either. The trio's manipulations lured many small shareholders to sell their stock when it went up and so more shares were available than Fisk and Gould had counted on having to buy. This last Erie affair marked the end of Drew's career as an important figure on

Wall Street. He went bankrupt in 1875 and when he died he was broke.

A tall, lanky man, Daniel Drew all his life looked and acted like a country bumpkin. He was ungrammatical in his speech and untrustworthy in his business dealings, as those who took his rural appearance at face value found out. When he built a large house on Union Square in New York City, he made sure the property included a cowshed and a horse barn. As he later wrote: "The smell of cattle now and then, particularly when he is cooped up in a city, sort of does a fellow good." Drew was almost obsessively pious in his religious worship. He "got religion" when he was a young man but declined to become a clergyman, saying: "There isn't much chance in preaching to get rich." He usually went to church twice on Sunday, to prayer meetings two nights a week, and prayed every day, regardless of what unscrupulous tricks he was trying to bring off on Wall Street. He paid for the building of a church on Fourth Avenue and also for one in his home town of Carmel, which became known locally and cynically as "St. Daniel Drew Church." He helped found a theological seminary in New Jersey, which was named for him when he promised to endow it with $250,000. In the end, the seminary never received the money but only the interest on that sum each year ($17,500, at seven percent) until Drew went broke when even that payment ceased. An old, disappointed but unrepentant man, Daniel Drew died in 1879.

Jim Fisk always put on a good show and always did things on a grand scale, whether in business or otherwise. He thought the Erie should have bigger and showier offices, so in 1869 he and Gould purchased Pike's Opera House at Eighth Avenue and Twenty-third Street, for $820,000. They probably used Erie money, but they put the building in their names and leased the upper floors to the railroad at $75,000 a year. They also spent $250,000 to renovate the offices, installing carved oak doors, marble washstands, thick rugs and silken hangings on the walls. Fisk's large chair and desk were on a raised dais. A safe was especially constructed, supposedly fireproof, that ran from the basement to the top floor, and was divided into individual safes on each floor. In the basement was the very useful printing press, handy when more stock had to be printed in a hurry.

The building also included a 2,600-seat theater, and so Fisk became a stage impresario as well as a railroad executive. He presented some of Shakespeare's plays, but also song-and-dance shows. On one occasion a corps of dancing blondes alternated with an equally attractive set of brunettes from night to night. Charles Francis Adams disapprovingly declared that Fisk had a "permanent harem." Not satisfied with one theater, Fisk leased two others, including the famous Academy of Music on Fourteenth Street. Some of his productions were commercial failures, but he never tired of having a spotlight played on him so he could take a bow after the final curtain went down.

Fisk also loved fancy clothes and gaudy uniforms and his best opportunity to wear them came in 1870 when he was asked to become colonel of the Ninth Regiment of the New York State National Guard. It was not that Fisk had any military experience, but the regiment was far below strength and had no decent uniforms or proper equipment. Its officers guessed, rightly, that Fisk would like the opportunity to dress up and lead a parade now and then and in return would put up the necessary money and supply the enthusiasm needed to revive the regiment. One of Colonel Fisk's first steps was to have designed and made for himself a uniform with much gold braid that was said to have cost two thousand dollars. He recruited new members, largely among Erie employees who could hardly refuse, and also formed, mostly from musicians who worked at his opera house, a first-class band.

On one occasion he took the whole regiment by boat, at his expense, to Long Branch, New Jersey, for a lively weekend at that resort. Another time he led his soldiers to Boston to participate in the celebration of Bunker Hill Day, but to do so he had to get the permission of the governor of Massachusetts, since Boston's mayor and other officials turned down his request. In 1871, however, Colonel Fisk found that soldiering was not all parades and excursions. The Ninth Regiment, along with others, was ordered to protect a parade in New York of Irish Orangemen (Protestants) who were certain to be opposed by their fellow Irish who were Catholics. When the parade got underway, shots were fired and bricks and stones thrown. The raw troops of the militia fired back, and among the dead when the riot ended were three members of the Ninth. Fisk tried to control his men but was trampled underfoot, suffering a dislocated ankle. Pursued by part of the mob, he escaped through a backyard and eventually reached a hotel. When the crowd caught up with him there, he fled again and did not stop until he was safe in Long Branch.

Fisk also fancied himself an admiral of sorts. When, in 1869, he bought a steamship line that ran between New York and Fall River, Massachusetts, he had a uniform designed that made him look like an admiral in the United States Navy. The costume included three silver stars on the coat sleeve, lavender gloves, and a large diamond breast pin. He wore this uniform when he welcomed President Ulysses S. Grant aboard one of his ships. If the president had looked, he would have found a canary in every stateroom, for Fisk was very fond of the little creatures. Fisk also had built a large ferryboat to operate on the Hudson and named it for himself. He hung two portraits of himself aboard it.

Jim Fisk was married when he was nineteen to a fifteen-year-old girl he had met in Brattleboro. The marriage lasted until Fisk's death, but the couple seldom saw each other. When Fisk first departed for the business and social excitement of New York, he left his wife, Lucy, in Boston. She occasionally visited him in New York, but for the most part stayed in Boston, where Fisk supported her in a very comfortable manner, showered her with gifts and apparently loved her. However, he also liked other female companionship and women were attracted to the jolly, generous stout man. Fisk's favorite for a number of years was Josie Mansfield (1842?–1931), of medium height, with thick black hair and full red lips, who claimed to be an actress. In 1869, Fisk set her up in a house half a block from the Erie opera house and offices. In a year or so, though, Josie became bored and dissatisfied, wanting even more money than Fisk was spending on her. She also met and was attracted to Edward (Ned) S. Stokes, a handsome, well-dressed man, six years younger than Fisk, who came from a well-to-do family but was usually in debt. Josie met him through Fisk, after the two men formed a company to run an oil refinery in Brooklyn.

To strike at his rival, Fisk canceled an arrangement between the refinery and the Erie, which was the only reason the refinery was profitable, and so wiped out Stoke's income, which he had done very little to earn. When Stokes collected $27,500 owed the refinery and kept it as his own, Fisk had him put in jail, and charged with embezzlement. Josie and Stokes, the former having deserted Fisk entirely, tried to blackmail Fisk by threatening to publish his letters to Josie. After many harsh words, an agreement was worked out covering both the dispute over the refinery and the letters. All was not settled, however, for in 1871 Josie sued Fisk for libel and on January 6, 1872, was on the witness stand to testify, while at the same time Fisk was asking that she and Stokes be indicted for blackmail. In the afternoon, Fisk went to the Grand Central Hotel on Broadway, where, while walking up a flight of stairs, he was shot twice by Stokes, standing at the top. Fisk died the next morning. He was buried in Brattleboro and a large monument was erected over his grave. Stokes was tried three times, finally convicted of manslaughter and sentenced to six years in jail.

Jim Fisk was a bulky, overweight man, with reddish blond hair and a large mustache, the latter waxed to a point at each end. He dressed in gaudy clothes, even when not in uniform, and liked lively parties, although he was not a heavy drinker. He had many friends and was generous with his money. The conservative, upper-class people of New York disliked him, not because of his business activities but because of his life-style. Those less well-off rather admired Fisk because he did not put on airs and got pleasure out of his money. Daniel Drew said Fisk was "as brisk as a bottle of ale"; the historian Henry Adams, though, said he was "coarse, noisy, boastful, ignorant," but admitted that his humor was truly American. In sum, he was like an enlarged photograph of the spirit of the times. When Fisk died, it was found he possessed only about $1 million of all the money that had passed through his hands, but his wife was worth about twice that amount.

Jay Gould, unlike Fisk, found no time for play. After 1868, Fisk had only a small role in Erie Railroad affairs, while Gould, in full control, tried to make it appear that the road was being improved. In fact, by 1871 the Erie was a physical wreck and it was badly in debt. Gould was attacked by the holders of Erie securities and in March, 1872, was ousted as president. Ironically, when the departure of Gould caused Erie stock to go up, he made $3.25 million from transactions in the stock. Gould, however, was charged with having stolen millions from the Erie treasury and was arrested for embezzlement. The charges were dropped when the new directors agreed to accept securities from Gould that he said were worth $6 million but that turned out to have a value of no more than $200,000.

Jay Gould's days as a railroad magnate, however, were far from over. Along with other ambitious men, who sometimes operated alone, sometimes in groups, he set out to control as much railroad mileage as possible. In doing so he became part of a chain of deals and mergers that took place in the latter years of the nineteenth century on such a scale and so frequently that it was difficult to be sure who controlled a given road at any particular time. Gould sought to control the Union Pacific Railroad by buying large blocks of stock. Reluctantly, the directors elected him to the board when he owned about a third of all the stock. With the backing of the financier Russell Sage (1815–1906), Gould acquired full control. He also went after the Kansas Pacific Railroad, which ran from Kansas City, Missouri, to Denver, Colorado, south of the Union Pacific. If he could acquire the Kansas Pacific stock cheaply, because it was in a bad financial situation, and then merge it into the Union Pacific, its stock would go up and he would gain several millions. He succeeded in early 1880, including in the merger the Denver Pacific Railroad.

Gould also attempted to combine and control all the important roads in the southwestern United States, including the Missouri Pacific and the Texas and Pacific, along with smaller lines. When the Texas and Pacific linked up with the Southern Pacific Railroad in 1882, a new transcontinental route came into service through the Southwest. In all his railroad dealings, Gould was not primarily concerned with the operation of the railroads. Rather, he manipulated stocks and used threats of extending one line into a competitor's territory in order to knock down the price of its stock or to force it into a merger.

In 1878, Gould moved into the Midwest by securing control of the Wabash Railroad, which connected St. Louis and the upper Mississippi region to the Great Lakes at Toledo. Some people saw this as a step toward creating an Atlantic-to-Pacific road, which would include the Erie. In any event, it put Gould in a position to play off other railroads in the East against each other because of the traffic he could feed them. Most of all, it brought a clash of interest between Gould and his backers and the Vanderbilt roads, now headed by the Commodore's son, William. William, showing he was not made of as stern stuff as his father, about this time felt obliged to sell some of the family's large holdings in the New York Central because of the pressure of public opinion. Gould managed to get in on the deal with the Morgan interests and so secured some of the stock. In other brushes between the two—as over depot facilities in Chicago—Vanderbilt was no match for the ruthless Gould.

Until 1879 Gould was mainly a manipulator of railroad stock and a consolidator of rail lines, but between 1879 and 1882, seven Gould roads built 4,231 miles of track, involving an investment of more than $84 million. He reached the peak of his career in 1881 when he controlled 15,854 miles of track, representing 15 percent of the nation's total. About two-thirds of the mileage was west of the Mississippi, but under his thumb he had lines as far east as Boston. Gould set up separate companies to do the construction work and made sizable profits out of them, too. He sometimes sold out his interest in a road if it was to his advantage to do so. In other cases he was ousted by security holders who had reasons for dissatisfaction with the way he was treating the property. By the summer of 1884, he controlled only three large systems: the Missouri Pacific, the Kansas and Texas, and the Texas and Pacific. An attempt to regain control of the Wabash in 1889 failed. Late in 1890, however, he did regain power over the Union Pacific. In December of that year, Gould participated in talks, organized by J. P. Morgan, aimed at ending the rate cutting by western roads that was hurting the profits of all of them. As usual, Gould caused difficulties. When one rate setting scheme collapsed in July 1892, a few months before his death, Gould was accused of being at fault by cutting charges on his lines.

It might seem that his many dealings in railroads, rather briefly summarized above, would have kept Gould busy, but such was not the case. Besides these activities, he managed to buy control of elevated railroads in New York City, to upset and then secure control of the nation's telegraph system, and at the same time engage in large-scale speculation on Wall Street, where one stock market operation caused more havoc and scandal than any other before or since.

In addition, Gould as one of the largest employers of the time, was one of the first of the Robber Barons to have to deal with large numbers of workers, who became more militant and better organized as the years went on. Gould was called to testify in 1883 before a Senate committee looking into the relations between labor and capital and expressed the opinion that unions should do nothing beyond educating their members and providing funds for widows and orphans. As to strikes, he asserted: ". . . they generally come from a class of dissatisfied men—the poorest part of your labor generally are at the bottom of a strike. Your best men do not care how many hours they work, or anything of that kind; . . . if men are temperate and industrious they are pretty sure of success."

Two years later Gould had to deal with a strike by organized labor, represented by the Knights of Labor. Blaming poor business conditions, many railroads, especially in the West, cut wages and discharged workers. Gould's Missouri Pacific fired several hundred. A strike led by the Knights tied up most rail traffic in the whole Southwest, with a good deal of sympathy shown toward them, largely because Gould was so widely hated. Gould offered to meet with union leaders, the first time anyone in his position had done so, and an indication that under the new conditions labor and capital might eventually bargain on equal terms. Gould agreed to restore the pay cuts.

The next year nine thousand employees of the Texas and Pacific went on strike and considerable violence followed, with widespread destruction of railroad property. Gould refused to run any trains because of the damage, and the public's sympathy turned against the Knights when it was deprived of transportation. Gould hired new workers and broke the strike. This victory for capital was a very damaging blow to the Knights of Labor and, coming about the same time as the Haymarket Riot, accelerated the decline of the union. Other railroad owners and industrialists took note of Gould's success and adopted his tough tactics.

Even while he was becoming the most important figure in railroading west of the Mississippi, Gould found time to seek, by his usual devious means, control of the elevated railroads of New York City. Here, too, he was aided by Russell Sage who was no more popular than Gould. At one time Sage was reputed to have $27 million out on loan, and when he died his estate was worth $70 million. There were three elevated railroad companies in New York, one of which was a holding company controlling the two operating companies. When Gould entered the picture in 1881, they were in bad condition financially, paid no dividends, and owed almost $1 million in back taxes. Nevertheless, the growing city made their future prospects bright, and the chance to make millions by stock manipulation was excellent. Gould used both legal weapons and publicity to gain control. Such actions as asking the courts to put one of the roads in receivership on the grounds that it was insolvent sent the price of its stock down, whereupon Gould and his associates bought at low prices. He also did his best to spread rumors and to plant stories in the newspapers that would reflect on the railways and their management. Gould, in this way, became a director of one of the roads in July 1882 and by 1884 controlled all the "els" in the city. As soon as control was assured, Gould doubled the fare from five cents to ten, but public reaction and that of some of the stockholders was such that he had to cancel the increase. In the end, the reorganization of the three lines and the growing demand for rapid transit made them extremely profitable.

Gould's tactics in seizing control of the nation's telegraph system were similar to those he had used in the elevated railway war. Western Union was by far the largest telegraph system and much of its strength was based on its exclusive contracts with many railroads, but it did not have a monopoly. As part of his dealings in Union Pacific affairs, Gould acquired the Atlantic and Pacific Telegraph Company. By 1877 this company had over seventeen thousand miles of wires and had become a serious rival to Western Union. The latter company then bought a large number of shares of its rival from Gould, but refused Gould a place on its board of directors. Gould took this as a social as well as a business snub.

Two years later, Gould entered the fray again by forming the Union Telegraph Company and putting up wires along the Wabash and another of his lines, where they duplicated the

Western Union lines. Gould also damaged Western Union by organizing bear raids on its stock to drive the price down, enabling him to acquire many shares at a low price. One of the leading stockholders of Western Union was William Henry Vanderbilt and, by early 1881, he had no stomach for further fighting with Gould, who by now was the largest stockholder. An agreement was reached by which Western Union took over the Union Telegraph by issuing more stock, some of which also went to other companies and individuals. In the end Western Union, in whose physical properties only about $25 million had actually been invested, had $80 million of securities outstanding. Before the end of 1881, Gould held a controlling interest in Western Union—about $30 million of its stock—and transferred his personal headquarters to the company's building in New York. The public's opinion of Gould was demonstrated in 1884 when he was accused of delaying the reporting of election returns over the Western Union wires in the very close presidential contest between Grover Cleveland and James G. Blaine so that he could gamble on the outcome. A crowd gathered at Western Union headquarters and threatened to hang Gould, who hastily telegraphed congratulations to Cleveland, as soon as his victory was certain.

Besides buying and selling railroads and telegraph systems, Gould found time for large-scale· speculations on the stock exchange and none was more spectacular—or more scandalous—than the gold conspiracy of 1869 that resulted in "Black Friday" on Wall Street. Gold could be bought and sold like any other commodity and its price rose and fell in relation to the American dollar. Exports were paid for by their foreign purchasers in gold so that if, for example, the dollar weakened, foreigners were able to buy more American wheat. This, Gould knew, would aid not only American farmers but also the railroads which would then carry more wheat. There was about $15 million worth of gold in circulation in the United States and, by the summer of 1869, Gould had bought nearly half of it in his scheme to drive up its value. His one fear was that the federal government might dump some of its $100 million worth of gold on the market if it thought the price went too high in relation to the dollar.

To avoid this disaster while he cornered the entire circulating supply, Gould tried to influence President Grant in two ways. In June he managed an introduction to the president and, on board Fisk's steamboat *Providence,* expressed to Grant his arguments as to why the price of gold should be kept high. Gould also induced Abel R. Corbin, Grant's brother-in-law, to try to influence the president and to keep Gould informed. In return, Gould opened an account in Corbin's name so that the latter would gain $15,000 every time gold went up a point. During July and August, with the aid of Erie funds and certified checks, which a bank he owned honored whether or not he had enough money on deposit to cover them, Gould bought between $30 million and $40 million in gold contracts. This meant that the various sellers were obligated to deliver to him two or three times as much gold as was available.

The plan worked well until the easygoing, inexperienced Grant was finally aroused and worried by Corbin's continual urging that he not let the Treasury put much gold on the market. Grant had his wife write Corbin's wife to tell her the Corbins must get out of gold speculation at once. Only Gould and Corbin knew of the letter and Gould, who now "owned" $50 million worth of gold, let his partner Fisk go on buying, thereby sending the price higher. On September 24—Black Friday—Gould knew the blow would fall any moment, so he quietly began selling his gold contracts at the then high price. When, shortly before noon, the Treasury announced it was putting $5 million of gold on the market, the price started to collapse and those who were still buying were trapped. An infuriated crowd of brokers forced Fisk and Gould to seek safety in the Erie Opera House, where they stayed for several days. Strangely, Fisk did not seem angry at his colleague who had misled him so badly. He repudiated his own gold contracts, saying a broker had bought them, not he. Gould did not care what was said about him for he had cleared $11 million in the process of disrupting the nation's money and stock markets.

Nevertheless, as a speculator in the stock market, Gould was not always successful. In 1884, for example, the market declined sharply and some of Gould's holdings—Missouri Pacific, Union Pacific, the Wabash, and Western Union—fell a great deal. At the same time, his many enemies saw a chance to squeeze him by driving down still further the prices of the stocks he held. Gould, on the verge of disaster, bluffed his way out. He threatened to declare bankruptcy, thus getting out of most of his obligations, unless his enemies helped him. They reluctantly decided it was to their own best interest to buy from him for cash fifty thousand shares of Western Union at a good price. Gould's stock dealings nearly ruined him although he seems to have had at the time an income of around $6 million a year from dividends and interest. At the end of December 1885, he announced he was retiring from Wall Street and even though his enemies did not believe it, he did. In 1890, two years before his death, Gould controlled the Missouri Pacific, the Manhattan elevated in New York, and Western Union, all of which were paying dividends, and he apparently had between $15 million and $20 million in cash, some of which he used to reacquire control of the Union Pacific.

Gould was also a newspaper owner for ten years and used the paper, the New York *World*, in an underhanded way to further his other interests. He acquired it in 1873 as part of a complicated deal involving chiefly the Texas and Pacific Railroad. When he was trying to win control of Western Union, he, who did his best to create monopolies, had the paper attack the telegraph company as an evil monopoly. He used the paper in similar fashion during the scheming for control of the elevated roads. His method in general was to have stories appear which ran down the credit of a company. This caused the stock to go down in price, Gould bought control, and then had the *World* praise the same company for its soundness.

When Jay Gould's business career came to an end, he was a very ill man. Always small and frail, with a full black beard and dressed in the dark clothes of the day, he made a cold and unimpressive appearance. Although he did not smoke or drink and ate sparingly, his health was never good. His death on December 2, 1892, was caused by tuberculosis. Gould was worth about $100 million when he died and all of it went to his family, none to worthy causes. In private life, the great speculator had been as straitlaced as he was unprincipled in his business career. His marriage was a happy one and he fathered six children. He had a mansion in New York and a large estate, Lyndhurst, at Irvington, on the Hudson, but he lived much less ostentatiously than other Robber Barons. At Lyndhurst he enjoyed especially his collection of orchids and other tropical flowers, which was the largest in the world.

Gould was without doubt the most hated of the Robber Barons. As soon as he died, stocks went up, especially those of Gould companies such as Western Union. Even fellow speculators disliked him personally. Vanderbilt would not socialize with Gould although the Commodore often played cards with Drew. The New York Yacht Club refused to admit Gould, and Mrs. Astor, leader of New York society, never invited him to her parties. Gould was interested in power and in money; he tried to outsmart other speculators for the pleasure of winning. The only benefit he bestowed upon the public resulted from his rate cutting wars with other railroad men and some of the railroad consolidation and construction which improved transportation facilities. Henry James wrote that he "was an uncommonly fine and unscrupulous intriguer," while crowds sang to the tune of "John Brown's Body," "We'll hang Jay Gould on a sour apple tree." In a case of the pot calling the kettle black, Drew said: "His touch is death."

Drew, Vanderbilt, Fisk, and Gould were by no means the only persons involved in this era in making dishonest fortunes out of railroads. While the quartet was busy ruining the Erie, other men on the other side of the continent were engaged in a project that thrilled the nation: the construction of the last two rail lines that would link the East and West Coasts. These men, too, were piling up fortunes in the process.

6

A Band of Iron

Many Americans dreamed of a transcontinental railroad from the time the nation first spread geographically from the Atlantic to the Pacific in the 1840's. Before the Civil War, however, the North and the South could not agree on a route to be followed, but this situation changed when the South seceded. Congress passed and President Abraham Lincoln signed on July 1, 1862, the Pacific Railroad Act. By the terms of this law, the Union Pacific Railroad was to build westward from Omaha, Nebraska, and the Central Pacific eastward from Sacramento, California. The law did not specify exactly where they were to meet. Each company was to receive ten alternate sections of 160 acres each of public land for each mile of track it built. In addition, each railroad was to be loaned by the government in the form of bonds, $16,000, $32,000, or $48,000 per mile; the amount depended on the difficulty of the terrain. Two years later, the amount of land to be given was doubled. The law encouraged a race between the two roads to see which could win the most land and the largest loans.

The Central Pacific Railroad was the corporate form assumed by four men who almost by accident were about to become railroad pioneers, to have a large part in making the dream of a transcontinental railroad come true, and to become very rich Robber Barons in the process. They were Mark Hopkins, Collis P. Huntington, Leland Stanford, and Charles Crocker. Hopkins (1813–78) was born the son of a storekeeper in New York State on

September 1, 1813. At fifteen he became a clerk in a village store and later had his own such business. He was with a firm of commission merchants in New York when news of the discovery of gold in California reached that city, and in January 1849 he combined with twenty-five other men in a joint venture to go west in search of gold. Hopkins never became a miner but instead set up shop to sell supplies to those seeking gold. Before long he met Huntington and in 1853 formed a partnership with him. The pair operated a very successful store in Sacramento.

Huntington (1821–1900) was born in Connecticut on October 22, 1821, the son of a rather incompetent farmer, and his education, only a few months a year, ended when he was thirteen. The next year he was apprenticed to a neighboring farmer for seven dollars a month and room and board. After that he spent a number of years as a peddler, a storekeeper, and in other occupations before he sailed from New York to California in March 1849. He took with him a stock of merchandise to sell and he bought and sold goods on the way so that he showed a profit of $3,800 by the time he reached San Francisco. There he worked hard and successfully, making sharp judgments as to what kinds of goods would sell best, until he moved his enterprise to Sacramento in 1851.

Stanford (1824–93) was born near Albany, New York, on March 9, 1824, the son of an innkeeper. He was well-educated and in 1848 was admitted to the bar. He moved to Wisconsin and opened a law office, but after four years he gave up his law practice and returned to New York. That same year he went to California, leaving his wife in the East for the time being, and following in the footsteps of four brothers who had already gone west. He set up a store in partnership with a friend in Cold Springs and in 1855 moved to Sacramento, where Hopkins and Huntington were already in business.

An easterner like the other three, Crocker (1822–88) was born at Troy, New York, September 16, 1822, and was educated at Rensselaer Institute. When his father went bankrupt in 1836, he took his family west to Indiana and Crocker began earning his own living, first as a farm worker, then in a sawmill. When he decided to go to California in 1850, he led a small band, including two of his brothers, overland. He had some success as a miner but in 1852 gave that up and went into storekeeping like the others. Also like the others, by the mid-1850's he was well-to-do and a leading citizen of Sacramento.

Besides being in business in the same growing city, the Big Four, as they came to be called, first found a common interest in politics. In 1856, two years after the Republican party was founded and the year it ran its first candidate for the presidency, Huntington became one of its strong supporters. With the split between North and South deepening over the issue of slavery, there was intense rivalry in the young state of California for political control between the long-established Democratic party and the new group. Crocker was elected to the state legislature in 1860 when Lincoln and the Republicans carried the state, but it was Stanford who became the important politician of the group. Although defeated when he ran for governor in 1859, he was selected to go east to Washington to see President-elect Lincoln about party matters in California. Two years later he was elected governor for a two-year term. Although he did not run for reelection, believing he would be defeated, his efforts and those of other Republicans were of material help in keeping California on the Union side when the Civil War broke out.

The Big Four first became interested in building a railroad to the east through a young engineer, Theodore D. Judah (1826–63). Born in Connecticut, Judah began a promising career even before he went to California in 1854. He built the Niagara Gorge Railroad and worked on the Erie Canal. He came to the West Coast to be the chief engineer of the Sacramento Valley Railroad, and soon began agitating for the construction of the western end of a transcontinental line, publishing a pamphlet on the subject in 1857. In November 1860, Judah called a meeting in Sacramento to promote his proposed line. Huntington and Crocker attended and the former became seriously interested. A little later he and Hopkins, with whom he had discussed the project at length, were among the first to put money into the scheme.

Plans progressed and on June 27, 1861, the Central Pacific Railroad was incorporated, with all of the Big Four now financially interested. They did not, however, get along well with Judah, who felt it was his road, since he had found a possible route through the Sierra Nevada, the rugged mountains running north and south in eastern California. By 1863, the Big Four were ready to ease him out, which they did for $100,000, and Judah, contracting a tropical fever while crossing the Isthmus of Panama, died soon after reaching New York.

Despite the general enthusiasm for such a railroad as the Central Pacific, it was difficult to find financing. At the start, only 1,580 shares were sold and on these only ten dollars each was paid down. Many who promised support backed out so that the Big Four came into control almost by default. Stanford was elected president and continued to hold the post while he was governor of the state, in which position his influence was useful. Ceremonies to mark the beginning of construction were held in January 1863, but no tracks were actually put down until October. By June 1864 the first thirty-one miles of the Central Pacific were ready to operate out of Sacramento. The Big Four found the whole project to be much more complex than they had thought. Nor did they yet realize that they were about to become national figures.

As was common practice at the time, the railroad itself did not manage the construction work but farmed it out to a company established for that purpose. Since both organizations were controlled by the same persons, this provided an excellent opportunity for large profits at the expense of other stockholders. In the case of the Central Pacific, Crocker took over the job of supervising the construction, although he was not an engineer. He was, however, a hard-working, energetic leader who turned in a remarkable performance. The arrangement for construction was made more formal—and more profitable—in 1867 when the four, along with Crocker's brother, Edwin, established the Contract and Finance Company. The Central Pacific agreed to pay this company $86,000 per mile of track built, half to be payable in cash and bonds, the other half in Central Pacific stock, valued then at only thirty cents on the dollar. The associates calculated that it would actually cost about $47,000 per mile to build the road and so they would gain $39,000 profit for every mile built. The profit depended, to some extent, on how valuable the stock became, since it was selling at a very low price at the time. As it turned out, costs in some places rose to about $64,000 a mile, so part of the potential excessive profit was lost.

To find the necessary cash to pay for materials and labor was not easy. Investors were shy about putting their money into a venture that could not earn a profit for several years at the least. The government land grants could not be sold to settlers until the railroad met the requirements of the law and acquired legal title. Huntington spent a good deal of his time in the East, trying to sell bonds and to secure credit from manufacturers whose supplies were needed. Altogether, about $36 million was spent building the Central Pacific. In return the road received government bonds and land grants with a stated value of about $38.5 million, but which were actually worth much less. In all, $54 million of Central Pacific stock was transferred to the construction company, and in time, when the stock went up in value, this was clear profit to the Big Four and Crocker's brother.

Except for the outrageous profit the associates made out of construction, the story of the building of the Central Pacific is an exciting one of men against nature. Most of the 742 miles that were eventually built ran through hilly or mountainous terrain so that by late spring 1865, only fifty-six miles had been built. In 1866, only twenty-six miles were completed and twenty-one the following year. Labor was in short supply and it was with great doubts that Crocker in 1865 hired fifty Chinese, believing them too small and frail to stand up to the hard work. They proved to be so hardworking and efficient that by 1867, 6,000 of them were at work and Crocker was importing more directly from China. Snowstorms in the mountains were another problem and it took as many as five locomotives together to push their way through drifts on the tracks. To keep the snow off the tracks, thirty-seven miles of snow sheds were built by 1869 at a cost of $2 million. Many tunnels had to be dug out of solid rock and many trestles built—one of them 878 feet long. It took nearly five years to reach the crest of the Sierras, and it was June 1868 before the California state line was reached. After that, construction was much easier and Crocker built 362 miles across the Nevada plains in 1868 and 1869, almost making good his promise of a mile a day.

While the Big Four were struggling with the financial and construction problems of the Central Pacific, and laying the groundwork for their fortunes, other men were building the Union Pacific westward to meet them—and making fortunes in an even more scandalous manner. The Union Pacific was organized in the fall of 1863 and in December ground was broken at Omaha to start construction. General John A. Dix (1798–1879), a New Yorker, was president but took no interest in the active management, which fell into the hands of Thomas C. Durant (1820–85). Durant was born in Massachusetts of colonial ancestry and was educated as a physician, but he found business and speculation more interesting. He helped build a railroad in Michigan before going west. During the construction of the Union Pacific, he was the most influential figure involved. He pushed hard to finish the line as soon as possible and he thereby added to the cost. Durant was influential in 1864 in persuading Congress to increase the land grants for the transcontinental roads.

Grenville M. Dodge (1831–1916), born in Massachusetts, was Crocker's counterpart on the Union Pacific after Dodge became its chief engineer in 1866. He had previously built railroads in Illinois and Iowa, and in the Civil War he was twice wounded and became a major general of volunteers. Construction work on the Union Pacific was much easier than it was on the Central Pacific and consequently the tracks were put down at a greater rate. By September 1866, 180 miles had been laid across the plains of Nebraska and by the end of the year the road was 193 miles west of Omaha. Construction became a race, since the amount of public land and government bonds earned was determined by the number of miles built. At the peak, the Union Pacific had about ten thousand men at work—Civil War veterans from both sides, ex-convicts, and Irish from New York—and was using about the same number of draft animals. In all, the Union Pacific built 1,038 miles of track.

By early 1869 both roads reached Utah and were building past each other on parallel lines because no decision had been made as to where they were to meet. After considerable arguing, with each side trying to get Congress to favor it, that body decided on Promontory Point, near Great Salt Lake. Trains from the two lines met there, cowcatcher to cowcatcher, on May 10, 1869, and a golden spike was driven into a cross tie to symbolize the fact that the nation was now bound together from the Atlantic to the Pacific by a band of iron. At first, trains took four and a half days to make the trip from Omaha to Sacramento and there was not as much traffic, either passenger or freight, as had been hoped. This disappointment was partly the result of the opening of the Suez Canal, between the Red Sea and the Mediterranean in November 1869. Freight that might have traveled between Asia and Europe across the American continent used this waterway instead.

The Union Pacific had its equivalent of the Central Pacific's Contract and Finance Company, the Crédit Mobilier of America, which not only made handsome profits for the insiders but also was involved in the bribery of members of Congress. The name, incidentally, came from that of a French firm that had made unusual profits out of public works. Durant was the organizer, in 1864, and first president of the Crédit Mobilier. Although the engineer who preceded the more complaisant Dodge estimated that the first hundred miles of track could be built for $30,000 a mile, Durant had the contract with the Crédit Mobilier made at $60,000 a mile. Durant lost control of this lucrative operation in 1867 and, in fact, was dropped as a director of the Union Pacific only fifteen days after the lines joined in Utah.

Durant's successor was Oakes Ames (1804–73), another native of Massachusetts, whose family owned the largest shovel factory in the country. As pioneers moved west, again when the gold rush miners in California needed tools, and in the early 1860's when the Union Army had to have shovels, the factory prospered tremendously. Ames served in the House of Representatives from 1863 to 1873 as a Republican, and after he and his brother gained control of the Crédit Mobilier, he used his legislative position to "sell" to other congressmen shares of that company, at prices much below their true value. He placed them "where they will do the most good," as he said—that is, to ensure favorable votes on railroad matters. These transactions did not come to public attention until 1872, when it was revealed that one of those who had received Crédit Mobilier shares under these terms was Schulyer Colfax, then vice-president of the United States, who had previously been speaker of the House of Representatives. Other members of Congress, including a future president, James A. Garfield, were implicated, but the only action taken was a vote of censure against Ames and another representative in 1873. Such were the ethics of the times, both in government and in business. The profit of the insiders who operated the Crédit Mobilier has been estimated at somewhere between $7 million and $23 million, all at the expense of the Union Pacific.

Even while the Central Pacific was being built, the Big Four were busy in California extending their control over as many of the state's transportation facilities as possible. At San Francisco and at Oakland, across the bay, they sought to acquire land and docking rights so as to keep any competitor out of the area. Purchase of the California Steam Navigation Company in 1869 gave them control over river traffic to the interior from San Francisco. Looking northward from Sacramento toward Oregon, the Big Four in 1868 won control of the California and Oregon Railroad. By the fall of 1869, Huntington, Stanford, Crocker, and Hopkins were powerful men, well on their way to controlling California's economic—and with it, political—destiny. In late September, just a few days after Jay Gould had brought about Black Friday on the gold market in New York, the Big Four were honored at a dinner in Sacramento for "the great enterprise which you inaugurated and carried through to triumphant conclusion." The leading newspaper of the city, however, called the Big Four "simply cold-hearted, selfish, sordid men."

Such language did not stop the four, who were already starting on the most extensive project of their careers, the building of the Southern Pacific Railroad. This line would comprise, within its system, railroad trackage that put an octopuslike grip on California. The Southern Pacific was organized in 1865 by a group of San Francisco men and the next year received a grant of land from Congress. It was to build a railroad south to San Diego and then east to the California-Arizona border, where it would connect with another railroad to form a new transcontinental line. Quietly and secretly the Big Four began buying stock of the Southern Pacific and by sometime in 1868 gained control. Now the new line, which its organizers had never been able to build, began moving south, although only eighty miles were constructed by 1870. In another seven years, though, seven hundred miles of tracks were laid and the Arizona border was reached.

The Southern Pacific was in a contest with the Texas and Pacific Railroad controlled by Thomas A. Scott (1823–81). He was a prominent railroad man for many years, was president of the Pennsylvania Railroad from 1874 to 1880, and of the Texas and

Pacific from 1872 to 1880. Scott wanted to have control of lines in California, not just to the Arizona border, and he and Huntington became involved in a hard-fought contest to influence Congress over rights of way. Huntington wrote: "I am fearful this damnation Congress will kill me," and reported that he was spending $200,000 to $500,000 each session to influence members of Congress. Huntington won the contest by getting an order from the federal government in 1877 that allowed the Southern Pacific to build across Arizona and New Mexico. Crocker put down three hundred miles of track in 1880 and the Southern Pacific in 1882 joined up with the Texas and Pacific near El Paso, Texas. As before, the associates made a great deal of money from the construction work. By February 1883, chiefly through Huntington's efforts, railroads in Texas and Louisiana were acquired so as to give the Southern Pacific a through route from San Francisco to New Orleans. Two years later the Big Four added steamships at New Orleans to complete a route all the way to New York.

Like warring medieval barons, the associates and their competitors often fought each other. In 1873 they and Jay Gould ran afoul of each other when Gould bought into the Pacific Mail Steamship Company at about the same time he acquired control of the Union Pacific Railroad. The Big Four organized a rival shipping company, the Occidental and Oriental, and Gould then agreed, for a share in the new company, to let the Pacific Mail resume a traffic-sharing arrangement with the Central Pacific. In 1887 the Southern Pacific and the Atchison, Topeka and Santa Fe Railroad engaged in a rate war when they could not agree on how to share California railroad traffic. The passenger rate from Chicago to San Francisco, when the transcontinental line opened in 1869, was $130. In March 1887, the roads cut the price to $32 and two days later set an all-time low rate of $1 for the trip from Kansas City to Los Angeles, a distance of 1,800 miles. Rates did not stay that low, but the war with the Sante Fe did encourage people to go west and the Southern Pacific carried 120,000 immigrants in a year.

The associates also became involved in 1880 in a conflict that ended in bloodshed with settlers along the route of the Southern Pacific. Several hundred settlers moved into the Mussel Slough district, now known as the Lucerne Valley, on land that the government had granted to the railroad. This land, however, had not yet been officially turned over to the Southern Pacific so it in turn could not yet give the farmers title to the land. They were assured they would get proper possession of their land for $2.50 an acre when the formalities were concluded. When the time neared, though, the road announced the price would be as high as $40 an acre and that outsiders would be allowed to bid on land already broken to the plow by settlers.

The farmers organized and tried to negotiate with Crocker and with Stanford. They also frightened one railroad land agent out of the area, but when a court upheld the railroad, the latter demanded that a United States marshal evict the settlers whose homes had been sold to outsiders. A marshal, supported by two armed railroad employees, turned up on May 11 and a gunfight broke out which resulted in eight deaths. Crocker got his side of the story to the newspapers first and so the public did not initially show the settlers the sympathy they might have. Seven of the farmers were indicted and five sentenced to jail. Others either met the railroad's terms or moved away. In the long run, though, sentiment turned against the railroad and this incident was one more factor in making the Southern Pacific and its rulers increasingly unpopular.

As the associates became more powerful and more disliked, they took several steps to protect their interests and to keep their monopolistic position in California. In 1884, under Huntington's leadership, they incorporated in Kentucky the Southern Pacific of Kentucky, a new holding company to own all their properties. Under the law, they could do this in such a way that any lawsuits in California would be heard in federal courts, not state courts, which Huntington feared would be prejudiced against them. Complaints against all the western railroads became so numerous that in 1887 President Cleveland, at the direction of Congress, appointed a Pacific Railway Commission. This body found that the Big Four had made more than $100 million on construction contracts alone. The Central Pacific Railroad and its subsidiaries, so the commission concluded, cost $58 million to build, but $62 million more than this had been paid out to the associates by their own votes as directors. Finally, the investigators calculated that about $2.25 million had been spent to influence legislators.

Stanford, who was considered by some to be an imposing public figure, made speeches on behalf of himself and his associates, and in 1872 they purchased a Sacramento newspaper in order to be able to answer another paper that was vigorously anti-Big Four. Although they argued strenuously for free competition—*laissez-faire* capitalism—what they really meant was that they did not want any government regulation. While they claimed that free competition among railroads would lower rates, they paid out about $26 million in rebates, subsidies, and pools in order to avoid that very competition which, temporarily at least, would benefit passengers and shippers.

Mark Hopkins was the first of the Big Four to die, passing away in a private railroad car at Yuma, Arizona, in March 1878 while there on an inspection trip. Hopkins was the quietest of the four and took a less active part in their work. Lacking about an inch and a half of being six feet tall, he was thin, and as he got older walked with a stoop. His face was long and thin and he spoke in a soft voice. Hopkins was thought by outsiders to be a miser and he was most austere in his eating and drinking habits. He hated waste and whenever he was out inspecting a rail line he picked up any bolts or spikes lying about. Eventually, though, he began building an ornate mansion on Nob Hill, overlooking San Francisco. He could well afford to considering, for example, that in 1874 the Big Four paid themselves a dividend of half a million dollars each out of railroad profits, and the next year one twice as large. The mansion had a dining room that seated sixty, while the master bedroom was finished in ebony, inlaid with ivory. The house was not quite completed when Hopkins died, leaving a fortune of at least $19 million. His widow finished the mansion, but lived mostly in the East and married a man twenty-two years younger than she.

Charles Crocker was a very large man who usually weighed over two hundred and fifty pounds. He had great energy most of the time, but occasionally had spells in which he refused to do anything at all. He was noisy and bossy, boastful and stubborn but certainly the best suited of the four to manage the construction work of their railroads. Rather abruptly in 1871, Crocker sold out to the others, although he continued to hold some Central Pacific stock. Two years later he changed his mind and resumed his former position in the organization. Shortly after this he, too, decided to build a mansion on Nob Hill and put up a large wooden structure that had a seventy-six-foot tower and cost about $1.5 million. When he could not acquire the whole block because one owner of a small lot refused to sell, Crocker had a fence, forty feet high, built around the offending property and home. Crocker constructed a luxurious resort at Del Monte where he died in August 1888. His fortune was estimated to be as high as $40 million.

Leland Stanford was the "front man" for the Big Four, the one who made speeches and who was active in politics all his life. He, too, was a large man, but unlike Crocker he was slow-moving and his mind also seemed to take its time before Stanford said anything. Some people thought he was a great statesman while others thought he was simply a figurehead whose speeches were full of very ordinary phrases and platitudes. In any event, he was an extremely successful man, in terms of both money and politics. His political career reached its climax in 1885 when he was elected United States senator from California. He was reelected six years later. He opposed the Interstate Commerce bill when it came before the Senate.

Stanford had more outside interests than his associates but he also built a mansion on Nob Hill. It was completed in 1876, next door to the Hopkins house, and cost $2 million. The glass-domed circular entrance hall was seventy feet high. In all there were fifty rooms. He acquired land south of San Francisco that eventually totaled over 8,000 acres, and here he became a very serious breeder of horses. By 1889 he owned 775 of them. In 1872 he hired a photographer to try to prove whether or not a trotter's four feet were ever all off the ground at the same time. Five years later some pictures were taken that proved this was so.

In the end, Stanford was remembered chiefly because he founded, in 1885, Leland Stanford, Jr., University, named for his son, an only child, who died of typhoid in 1884 in his sixteenth year. Mr. and Mrs. Stanford founded this university in his memory, giving it about $5 million worth of land as an initial endowment. Stanford University welcomed its first students in the fall of 1891, and Stanford left it $2.5 million when he died in

1893. His estate was estimated to be worth anywhere from $50 million to $100 million, but it may have been somewhat less. In any event, Mrs. Stanford's diamonds were worth $1 million, not counting other jewelry.

Collis Huntington, the last of the Big Four to die, not only carried on business operations longer than the others but also was involved in a variety of projects without them. He made New York his headquarters and there he had his own mansion, costing $2.5 million and comparing well in extravagance with the houses of the others on Nob Hill. Huntington's first connection with an eastern railroad, the Chesapeake and Ohio, came about in 1869 but it was not until 1878, with the line in receivership, that he formed a syndicate to secure control. Huntington embarked on a program of expansion, building more miles of track and turning Newport News, Virginia, into an important seaport. From here his ships sailed to England, to South America, and up the navigable Virginia rivers. Crocker and Stanford were associated with him in one project to join the Chesapeake and Ohio to the Southern Pacific at New Orleans. In 1884 Huntington thereby became the only person who owned or controlled railroad lines all the way from the East coast to the West coast, although it was a rather roundabout route. He established a shipbuilding company at Newport News in 1887 and by 1895 was building battleships for the Unites States Navy.

A feud broke out between Huntington and Stanford in 1885 that embittered their relations from then on. Huntington thought Stanford had agreed to support for the Senate a candidate favorable to their railroad interests, but Stanford, without telling Huntington, changed his mind and decided to seek the seat himself. Huntington waited five years for revenge when, in 1890, he insisted that Stanford step down as president of the Southern Pacific, to be replaced by Huntington. This was not only done, but Huntington also publicly turned on his former friend and charged that Stanford's seat in the Senate had been bought with railroad money used as bribes.

Huntington, too, was a large man, over six feet tall and weighing two hundred pounds. He had a big, round head and a commanding presence. He was full of energy and had a shrewd mind but he cared for nothing except the success of his plans, no matter what dishonesty or harm to the public might be involved. In one instance, Huntington saw to it that Senator William Stewart of Nevada received fifty thousand acres of land in the San Joaquin Valley for his services in supporting the railroad men in Congress. The man who was, overall, the nation's greatest railroad builder was described by an anonymous commentator as "scrupulously dishonest."

Huntington died in August 1900 at his camp in the Adirondack Mountains in northern New York State. Many estimates were forthcoming as to the size of his fortune and it probably was at least $40 million. Most of it went to his widow and his nephew, Henry E. Huntington, and in 1913 these two married. One result of this union was the establishment, with the uncle's money, of the world famous Henry E. Huntington Library and Art Gallery in San Marino, California.

While the Big Four were building a railroad empire in California and the Southwest, and for some time afterward, other men with similar talents and ambitions were bringing railroad tracks and their related financial manipulations to the Northwest—that great expanse of land lying between the western Great Lakes and the Pacific coasts of Washington and Oregon.

7

Northwest Passage

As the Big Four dominated the railroads of California and part of the Southwest for years, so did similar men rule the roads of the Northwest. They engaged in battles for the control of lines and, in the usual ways, accumulated, and sometimes lost, fortunes. One of these men, in fact, came near to winning control of most of the rail lines west of the Mississippi. These would-be monopolizers were Henry Villard (1835–1900), James J. Hill (1838–1916), and Edward H. Harriman (1848–1909).

Villard was born Heinrich Hilgard in Bavaria on April 10, 1835, and changed his name in the United States, to which he migrated in 1853. His father was a well-to-do lawyer, later a judge, and Villard studied law in Germany. He arrived in New York with no money and no knowledge of English but he had relatives in the United States who took him in. After studying law again and selling books from door to door, Villard began the career in which he first made a name for himself—journalism—in Racine, Wisconsin, where he was hired to edit a short-lived German-language newspaper for antislavery Republicans. While doing so, he practiced writing English several hours a day. In 1858 he covered the political debates between Abraham Lincoln and Stephen A. Douglas. (At the time he thought Lincoln an "uncouth, common Illinois politician," but later he concluded that he was "one of the great leaders of mankind.") As a war correspondent during the Civil War, Villard was present at such engagements as Bull Run, Shiloh, and Fredericksburg. In 1866 he married Fanny Garrison, the only daughter of the controversial abolitionist leader, William Lloyd Garrison.

Villard became involved with American railroads in February 1873 while in Germany recovering from a stroke. Some German holders of bonds in the Oregon and California Railroad Company asked him to go to Oregon to determine whether or not their investment was a sound one. He did so in 1874, and found, among other things, that a road which had issued $3 million of bonds had not built a single mile of track. But he also became extremely enthusiastic about the future of Oregon and made known he was prepared to move there and become the active manager of the properties in question. As a result, in 1876 he was elected president of the Oregon and California Railroad and the Oregon Steamship Company. He was also named receiver for the bankrupt Kansas and Pacific Railroad.

Villard's ambitions increased and in 1879, with the backing of a group of investors, he formed the Oregon Railway and Navigation Company from two steamship companies and one small railroad. The charter of the new organization empowered it to build railroads in Oregon, Washington, Idaho, and Utah. A year later, Villard announced that 115 miles of track along the Columbia River were nearly ready, and in 1880 he formed the Oregon Improvement Company which dealt in coal mines, agricultural land, and other ventures. Villard also found time and energy that year to direct both the financial and the engineering efforts of the Oregon and California Railroad to complete its line to the California border.

The major work of Villard's career, however, was the building of the Northern Pacific Railroad, although he had no connection with it at its start. The line was chartered in 1864 to be a second transcontinental road, running from Lake Superior to a port on the Pacific in Washington. The road was to receive forty alternate sections of public land for each mile completed in the territories it crossed and twenty sections per mile in the areas that were states of the Union. In all, the line stood to gather in forty million acres across Minnesota, North Dakota, Montana, Idaho, and Washington, with a connection to Oregon. Financial support was hard to secure and it was 1870 before any rails were laid, but nearly five hundred miles were completed in the next three years. Then the panic of 1873 struck, the banking house of Jay Cooke, which had been financing the road, went bankrupt, and Congress, shaken by the Crédit Mobilier scandal, could not be expected to provide any further aid. Construction came to a halt for several years.

Villard, still enthusiastic about the potential of the Northwest, decided to try to get control of the Northern Pacific. If completed, it would link up with his present transportation system, which had a practical monopoly at the Pacific end of the Far West. Villard was now so highly thought of that he was able to raise $8 million among friends and investors who subscribed this amount without being told what it would be used for. Against opposition, Villard bought Northern Pacific stock and in 1881 gained control of the road. He was determined to push the line and its branch roads to completion as soon as possible by building 2,000 miles of track in two years. At the height of the work, 25,000 men, of whom 15,000 were Chinese, were laboring and the construction cost was $4 million a month. Formal ceremonies to mark the completion of the road were held west of Helena, Montana, on September 3, 1883. Among those present were 2,000 Indians, some of whom performed war dances. President Chester A. Arthur and General Ulysses S. Grant had been present at an earlier ceremony in Minneapolis, Minnesota.

Villard's triumph was short-lived. The Northern Pacific incurred a very large debt because of construction costs, although Villard had not bled off money for inflated building charges as others had done. The road also ran through some of the least settled areas of the country so that it would be a while before any large amount of traffic could be expected. In addition, an associated company, the Oregon and Transcontinental, of which he was also head, was on the verge of bankruptcy. To add to Villard's burdens, the West Shore Railroad in New York, in which he had invested heavily, collapsed. Villard sadly resigned his presidency of both the western companies in December 1883. Since the fall in value of the stocks involved caused many persons heavy losses, Villard was blamed, although he suffered greater losses than anyone. Some people were incensed when he moved into an imposing mansion on Madison Avenue, in New York, just as his railroad empire collapsed. The truth was, he had started the home when he seemed well able to afford it and now had nowhere else to go. In a state of nervous exhaustion, Villard moved out of the city in the spring of 1884 and never again lived in his mansion.

A new crisis in the Northwest was threatened in 1887 when the Oregon and Transcontinental ran into financial trouble as it attempted to gain control of the Northern Pacific by buying large numbers of shares. Villard was now representing a German bank in the United States for the purpose of investing funds from that country and, when approached, he agreed to reenter the railroad arena. He became a director of the Northern Pacific and in 1888 resumed the presidency of the Oregon and Transcontinental. Villard found himself involved in a complicated financial contest with the Union Pacific for control of companies he was interested in and in 1889 accepted the chairmanship of the Northern Pacific. In this position he managed the sale of $160 million of bonds, partly to refinance earlier borrowings and partly to make improvements in the road.

As in 1883, however, fortune was not long on Villard's side. His broker, who handled large transactions for him, failed in 1890 and this helped cause the collapse of the North American Company, which was the successor company to the Oregon and Transcontinental. Again, Villard was blamed for the losses. If he deserved to be blamed, it was for the common fault of overoptimism which had led to the splurge of railroad building in the West, almost all of it on borrowed money. In June 1893 Villard resigned the chairmanship of the Northern Pacific. Two months later the road went into bankruptcy once more and Villard, although asked, declined to try to rescue it.

Villard restored his personal fortune between 1883 and 1890, partly by railroad operations but also through his other business activities. He showed an early interest in the use of electric power and in 1889 was one of the founders of the Edison General Electric Company. He served as president until 1893. Villard's interest in journalism led him to buy the New York *Evening Post* and the magazine the *Nation* in 1881. Spurred by his enthusiasm for the Northwest, Villard worked hard to attract immigrants from the East and from Europe and these efforts were, of course, to the benefit of his railroad operations. He established an office in

Boston in 1874 to sell land, and other agencies were opened in England and Scotland. German-language booklets were distributed in his native land. To this extent, and in his general promotion of the Northwest, Villard was working for the common good. At the same time, though, he was one of a group of financiers and railroad promoters, all of whom vied for control or monopoly of transportation lines, amid equally fierce rivalry among the new cities of the region. As a result, Villard and the others built too many miles of track too soon and the resulting collapse in the value of stocks and bonds injured thousands of investors in the United States and abroad. He did, indeed, make a large fortune out of the railroad boom of the late nineteenth century, but none of it seems to have been acquired in the dishonest manner of those involved in the Crédit Mobilier, for example.

The other major builder of railroads in the Northwest, James J. Hill, was a considerably different kind of man from Villard. Born in the province of Ontario, Canada, on September 16, 1838, Hill received the equivalent of a high school education, then went to work as a grocery store clerk at four dollars a month when his father died. After four years he left home and in July 1856 arrived in St. Paul, Minnesota, a small but rapidly growing city. Here he found a job as a clerk in a steamboat agency where he showed such energy that he was soon virtually running it. When the Civil War began he tried to enlist but was turned down because a boyhood accident had cost him the sight of one eye. By the end of the war, Hill was in business for himself as a general transportation agent, busy with many shipping projects. He introduced coal into the area for home heating and industrial use and made a very profitable business of it. One local newspaper remarked that "Jim Hill has a habit of securing things when he goes after them." He had his own steamboat operating on the Red River in 1871. Hill's travels made him well acquainted with a large part of Minnesota; bad weather and hardship did not bother him. During one blizzard he set the broken arm of a companion.

Hill was not only looking around the country. He was also looking into the future where he saw the triumph of railroad transportation. When the St. Paul and Pacific Railroad went bankrupt, like many others in the Panic of 1873, Hill seized the opportunity. With the aid of some associates, including a Canadian banker, he secured control of the line in March 1878, taking the place of Dutch investors who had lost nearly $14 million. The road consisted of slightly fewer than 300 miles of track, but had a land grant totaling more than five million acres. Hill moved fast to lay down more tracks, both to create business and to meet the terms of the St. Paul's charter. By December 1878, with Hill out on the line a good deal of the time encouraging the workers, the road reached the Canadian-American border. At about the same time, the Canadians completed a railroad south from Winnipeg to the border, which enabled Canadian grain to be transported to the East over United States lines. Meanwhile Minnesota was growing and its annual wheat crop was bigger every year. All of this meant good business for Hill's first railroad venture.

His Canadian background and the success of the St. Paul resulted in Hill joining the executive committee of the Canadian Pacific Railway in 1880, the same year he became an American citizen. The road had been chartered in 1873 and was intended eventually to be Canada's transcontinental line, although to begin with, it was to run only from Lake Superior to the West Coast. Work had bogged down, partly as the result of a scandal much like that of the Crédit Mobilier. Hill took over responsibility for the route of the road and for construction. In the fifteen months from June 1882, 675 miles were built, and the line was completed in 1885. Hill, however, resigned as a director in 1883, since the Canadian Pacific competed with his own line and with his interest in building another transcontinental road in the United States.

Hill slowly but steadily expanded his rail lines, buying control of some short lines and always pushing westward. In 1889 the system became known as the Great Northern. It ran north of the Northern Pacific, except in Minnesota, and its West Coast terminal was Seattle, Washington. In 1884 Hill's road consisted of 1,307 miles of track in Minnesota and North Dakota. Three years later, 8,000 men and 3,300 teams of horses were at work grading the 550-mile route from Minot, North Dakota, to Great Falls, Montana. By 1888 the tracks reached Helena and Butte, Montana, the latter providing copper to be shipped on the new road. Hill prevailed on Congress to pass a law allowing the Great Northern to run its tracks across Indian and military reservations.

The road was completed in 1893, and in July through passenger service between St. Paul and Seattle, a distance of 1,816 miles, began. Hill also built many miles of branch lines to act as feeders for the main road. The Great Northern was constructed without a government subsidy of any kind and was one of the few western railroads that did not go bankrupt as a result of the Panic of 1893. James J. Hill was a sound railroad builder and the Great Northern was his own creation every mile of the way.

Like most of the other Robber Barons, Hill was involved in a variety of enterprises, most of them connected with his railroad operations. He carried out agricultural experiments and offered the results to farmers because this would increase freight traffic. He bought high quality bulls and cows in Great Britain and distributed them free to selected farmers. He also sent out a train over the Great Northern to demonstrate to farmers new methods in animal and vegetable culture. He kept some freight rates low in order to make western timber, for example, competitive in price in the east, while he charged immigrants from Europe only ten dollars for rail fare to the Northwest if they would settle along his lines.

Hill was also interested in increasing American trade with the Far East so that the Great Northern would carry more freight. To do this he founded a steamship company which introduced American cattle, New England textiles, and Minnesota flour to Japan. Hill once calculated that if the people of one Chinese province consumed an ounce of American flour a day they would require fifty million bushels of wheat a year. Other ventures brought more immediate returns. With no great enthusiasm he bought some lumber property in Minnesota because it might possibly have iron ore underneath. It did and, as part of the rich Mesabi Range, was extremely profitable.

Edward H. Harriman, who was to be Hill's greatest rival and engage him in one of the wildest financial battles of the period, was born in Hempstead, Long Island, on February 25, 1848. He was the son of a not very successful Episcopal clergyman who served in a rather large number of different churches. Although he did not have to leave school, Harriman decided to do so when he was fourteen to accept a job at five dollars a week as office boy with a Wall Street broker. He was bright, ambitious, and a fast learner. By the time he was twenty-two he had his own firm and a seat on the stock exchange, aided in this rapid progress, according to rumor, by being one of the few traders to make money out of Jay Gould's 1869 conspiracy to corner gold. By the time he was thirty, Harriman had a small fortune, having already proved himself one of the shrewdest traders Wall Street ever knew.

Harriman first became interested in railroads through his father-in-law, who was president of a small road in northern New York. In 1881 Harriman and some associates bought a small line in north central New York and two years later Harriman became sole owner. The road was losing money, but by improving its equipment and showing what could be done with it, he was able to sell it to the Pennsylvania Railroad at a handsome profit. This and other dealings in small railroad properties gave Harriman an appetite for venturing into the ownership and management of larger railroads. He had, in fact, begun to buy stock of the Illinois Central Railroad in 1881. This line, which when completed in 1856 took the title of longest railroad in the world with its 800-mile long main track, was a successful Midwestern road. Harriman's interest was caused initially by his friendship with Stuyvesant Fish, a member of a wealthy New York family, who had become active in the management of the Illinois Central. After being elected a director in 1883, Harriman pushed strongly for expansion and within five years the road's trackage increased by one thousand miles as the result of the acquisition of smaller lines. Harriman had his first brush with the power of the banker J. P. Morgan in 1886 and 1887, when they fought for control of a railroad in Iowa that had been leased to the Central. The Harriman side won on a technicality when Morgan tried to vote some of his shares by proxy, which was illegal in Iowa. During the first ten years that Harriman was a director of the Illinois Central, it added more than fifteen hundred miles of track and increased its annual earnings from under $9 million to $20 million.

The expansion of the Illinois Central was Harriman's first important success in the railroad business, but it was his acquisition and revival of the Union Pacific that showed he had real genius in this field. The road was bankrupt in 1893. One group of investors that tried to get control of it was headed by Jacob H. Schiff (1847–1920) of the banking firm of Kuhn, Loeb and

Company. Schiff was born in Germany and came to the United States in 1865. He was so successful as a broker that when he was only thirty-eight he became head of the firm. Besides his business interests, Schiff was active in philanthropies, aiding the education of blacks in the South and endowing the Jewish Theological Seminary in New York. Schiff's group ran into strong opposition in its attempt to buy the Union Pacific, and the opposition turned out to be coming from Harriman. Harriman made peace with Schiff when he was promised a place on the executive committee, and thereafter the two men were associated in other operations of this kind, especially in financial battles with groups headed by J. P. Morgan.

The new owners took over in early 1897. Although he was well-off at the time, Harriman's large fortune grew out of his management of the Union Pacific. In 1898, after an almost step-by-step observation trip over the line, Harriman convinced the directors that $25 million should be spent on improvements. The Oregon Short Line Railroad, which gave another connection to the Pacific in Oregon, was reacquired for the Union Pacific in 1899 and $6 million was spent to improve it. The total mileage of the system went up from 2,848 miles to 5,391. As early as 1898 a small dividend was paid and by 1906 annual earnings increased to $47 million. Harriman proved himself not only a clever financier but also an efficient manager.

His connection with the Chicago and Alton Railroad also showed his shrewdness and his managerial ability, but did not reflect any credit on his business ethics. The Chicago and Alton was a prosperous line in 1898, although its tracks and equipment needed improvement. Harriman and others, including Jay Gould's son, George Jay Gould (1864–1923), the Kuhn, Loeb banking house, and James Stillman, head of the National City Bank of New York, bought a large part of the stock and by early 1899 controlled the road. As soon as this syndicate had control, it sold itself $40 million of bonds at a low enough price so that it could resell them to the public and make a profit of $8 million, which should have gone to the railroad. The next step was to declare a dividend of nearly $7 million, which put about a third of the receipts of the bond sale into the hands of Harriman and the other insiders. As usual, Harriman saw to it that the road was improved physically, but in seven years, while the capitalization was increased by over $80 million, only $18 million went into improvements.

Not long after Harriman achieved control of the Union Pacific, he realized that it could accomplish only so much on its own because the Central Pacific, running the rest of the way to the West Coast, was in other hands. As soon, therefore, as Collis Huntington died in 1900, Harriman and his backers began to seek control of the Southern Pacific, of which the Central Pacific was a part. Harriman persuaded the Union Pacific directors to authorize a bond issue of up to $100 million to be used in acquiring the system the Big Four had built. Despite opposition, he was successful by the early part of 1901. As usual, Harriman made many physical improvements, including shortening the Central Pacific by about fifty miles by better engineering of its route. On the Southern Pacific itself he spent $20 million. In the process of improving the Southern Pacific, Harriman clashed with the Atchison, Topeka and Santa Fe for a route through a canyon in Arizona. He offered to compromise and suggested that each line let the other put two representatives on its board of directors. When the Santa Fe refused, Harriman bought enough shares of it so that he had the votes to elect two directors of his choice.

With both Harriman and Hill expanding their railroad empires in the West, an eventual collision, much like two locomotives meeting head on, was inevitable. Both wanted to carry as much of the traffic to and from the Pacific Coast as possible and both wanted control of a railroad that would give them access to the rail center of Chicago. Also, Hill and his associates, who included J. P. Morgan, in 1896 gained control of the Northern Pacific, thus putting both of the northwestern transcontinental lines in the same hands. The stage was now set for a clash between Harriman and Hill for control of the Chicago, Burlington and Quincy Railroad, which had an eastern terminus in Chicago. It was also a large enterprise, with 7,911 miles of track, much of which lay in the area between the Missouri River and Denver and hence was in competition with Harriman's Union Pacific. Harriman in 1900 began to buy Burlington stock, but by the end of the year he gave up because not many holders cared to sell to him. Hill and Morgan got the jump on Harriman the next year when they induced the directors of the Burlington to sell out to them.

Harriman then entered into a bold scheme to get control of the Burlington by buying enough shares of the Northern Pacific to dominate that line and so indirectly have the Burlington. Northern Pacific stock outstanding, common and preferred together, was worth $155 million, of which the Hill-Morgan group held about one-fifth. Using Union Pacific funds, Harriman, with Schiff managing the operation, acquired more than half the common stock and nearly half the preferred before Hill and Morgan realized what was happening. Hill at this time was in Seattle and had a special train assembled to carry him to New York as fast as possible. Morgan, meanwhile, was on vacation in France and, by cable in early May 1901, authorized the purchase of fifteen million shares of Northern Pacific common. A struggle then began in which the two sides in their mad rush to buy control drove the price of the stock as high as $1,000 a share. The furious contest drained so much cash into dealings in the one stock that other stocks plunged downward and the New York Stock Exchange was in a state of panic as values were wiped out. In the end those who sold Northern Pacific short, hoping to make fortunes, found that there were not enough shares available to cover their promised deliveries. Coming to their senses, the Harriman and Hill groups allowed the shorts to settle for $150 a share and order was restored. Morgan and Hill were permitted to name the directors of the Northern Pacific, but Harriman and William Rockefeller, a brother of oilman John D., were given places on the board and Harriman became a Burlington director as well.

Later in 1901 Hill and Morgan proposed a scheme they thought would protect their interests in the Great Northern, the Northern Pacific, and indirectly in the Burlington. They formed the Northern Securities Company as a holding company and this concern exchanged its stock for that of the three operating roads. The company was capitalized at $400 million. Hill headed the concern and his group named ten of the fifteen directors, but Harriman's stake in the enterprise came to $82.5 million worth of stock. This plan brought peace between the railroad rivals, but in

March 1902 President Theodore Roosevelt ordered the Justice Department to bring suit against Northern Securities for violating the Sherman Antitrust Act.

Morgan, feeling his financial empire should deal on equal terms with the United States, proposed to the president that they let Morgan's lawyers and the attorney general of the United States get together and reach a gentlemanly agreement. Roosevelt rejected this proposal, and in March 1904 the Supreme Court, by the narrow margin of five to four, agreed that Northern Securities violated the law and ordered it dissolved. The court's decision resulted in acrimonious disagreement and legal action as to how the assets of the dissolved company were to be disposed of, and the result was not to Harriman's satisfaction. In the long run, though, when Harriman sold the stock he received in 1905 and 1906 from the dissolution, the Union Pacific showed a net gain of about $58 million.

Hill and Harriman later engaged in battles over rail routes in Oregon and Washington in which rival building crews fought with dynamite as well as fists and in which constant legal disputes were carried on. Hill formally resigned as president of the Great Northern in 1907 and his son Louis became the head, but the older Hill remained active. He was a director of a number of banks and in 1912 bought control of two banks in St. Paul. Two years later he had construction started on a fourteen-story building in St. Paul to be the headquarters of the Great Northern.

Physically, Jim Hill was not tall but was powerfully built, with broad shoulders and he remained for most of his life the vigorous, outdoor type. On one occasion he relieved a freezing railroad workman who was shoveling snow after a blizzard so that the man could get warm. On another occasion, when the people of a village in Minnesota complained of the noise Hill's trains and trainmen made, he had the town's depot torn down and rebuilt two miles away. A Protestant himself, he gave a million dollars to found a Catholic theological seminary because he thought one would be beneficial to the area. He gave three quarters of a million dollars to St. Paul for a public reference library.

Hill became a collector of paintings and was among the first Americans to appreciate the French Impressionists. He also greatly admired Napoleon Bonaparte and attributed his own success to: "Work, hard work, intelligent work, and then some more work." His railroad operations were efficient but the profits were very great and many struggling farmers along the Great Northern felt freight rates were far too high. They had a saying: "After the grasshoppers we had Jim Hill." There was also a ditty about the empire builder that went: "Twixt Hill and Hell, there's just one letter;/Were Hill in Hell, we'd feel much better." Hill died in May 1916 leaving an estate worth $53 million.

Harriman also carried on many activities to the end of his life. He began in 1905 planning a transportation system that would encompass the earth. This grandiose scheme called for an American shipping line across the Pacific to Japan, control of railroads in Manchuria, Siberia, and European Russia, and, finally, another steamship line from the Baltic Sea to the Atlantic Ocean and on to the American East Coast. Harriman made a trip to Japan in 1905 to try to acquire the South Manchurian Railway, but complications arising out of the war between Japan and Russia caused the deal to fall through. Harriman did not give up. As late as the year in which he died, 1909, he was working on plans to build a new rail line across part of China to the Siberian border. In 1902 he conceived the idea of building a railroad line in Mexico and secured permission to do so. His many other interests, however, took precedence and it was 1909 before he put his plan into action. In July, two months before he died, he made an inspection trip along the first eight hundred miles of this Mexican line.

Despite his business interests which ranged over much of the world, Harriman found time for activities of a different kind. He was prominent in politics on behalf of the Republican party, contributing large sums of money so that he was for a while considered the Republican "boss" of New York State. After a period of close relations with Theodore Roosevelt, Harriman and the president had a falling out over several misunderstandings. In a letter Roosevelt termed Harriman an "undesirable" citizen. This was in late 1906 and about the same time, whether by coincidence or not, the Interstate Commerce Commission began to investigate some of Harriman's earlier business activities. Harriman, in turn, blamed Roosevelt for the Panic of 1907.

Under Harriman's leadership a boys' club was founded in Manhattan in 1876, and the then young broker spent many hours promoting it and working with the boys. He paid most of the cost of $185,000 in 1901 for a new building. Deciding he needed a long rest in 1899, he chartered a steamer and took to Alaska not only a large party of family and friends, but also twenty-five scientists and five photographers and artists. On one occasion Harriman tramped for sixteen miles over a glacier. The expedition brought back a great deal of valuable scientific information. When the San Francisco earthquake nearly destroyed that city in April 1906, Harriman ordered his railroads to give all help possible and the next day he set out from New York on a special train to take personal charge. The Southern Pacific and Central Pacific supplied food, moved nearly a quarter of a million people out of the stricken city and, in all, brought 1,603 carloads of supplies, free of charge, into the city in thirty-five days.

Like most of the Robber Baron millionaires, Harriman built a large and costly home, but in his case he selected a hilly, wooded area on the west side of the Hudson River, about an hour and half on the Erie Railroad from New York City. Eventually the estate totaled twenty thousand acres, and on top of one of the hills Harriman erected a magnificent home in which all the materials and workmanship were American at his insistence. It was, however, not completed until the summer of 1909, so he had only two months to enjoy it. Harriman left his fortune of $100 million to his wife, and many thousands of acres of the estate went to New York State for park use.

Edward H. Harriman was a small, unimpressive but sharp-eyed man with a drooping mustache. He did not make friends easily and often rubbed people the wrong way. As a businessman he was described as shrewd, cool, greedy, autocratic, and ruthless. He was all of these, but he also was driven to do things because others said they could not be done. Along with his striving for power and money, Harriman paid equal attention to the physical aspects of the railroads he controlled. On one occasion, for example, he determined that if the track bolts used on the Southern and Union Pacific railroads were shortened a bit a total of fifty million ounces of iron could be saved.

During 1906 and 1907, Harriman invested $130 million of Union Pacific funds in the stock of nine other railway companies, whose lines reached into all parts of the country, north and south, east and west. He was accused of wanting to control all railroad traffic in the country, or at least to monopolize transcontinental railroading. Perhaps he did, but as wide as his interests were, he was far from achieving such a goal, although by 1906, when American rail trackage was nearing its all-time peak, the Harriman interests and six other groups did control nearly two-thirds of the 225,000 miles of track, in the following alignments:

The Harriman lines, 25,000 miles, made up mainly of the Union Pacific, the Southern Pacific, and the Illinois Central;

The Vanderbilt roads, 22,500 miles, which included the New York Central and the Chicago and Northwestern;

The Pennsylvania Railroad group, 20,000 miles, which in addition to the parent line included the Baltimore and Ohio and the Chesapeake and Ohio;

The lines in which J. P. Morgan was the dominating figure, 18,000 miles, including the Erie, the Southern Railroad, and other lines in the South;

The Gould roads, 17,000 miles, now managed by Jay's son George, based on the Missouri Pacific and other lines in the Southwest;

The Rock Island system, 15,000 miles, which was important in the Mississippi Valley and was assembled by William H. Moore;

Finally, the Hill roads, 21,000 miles, the core of which was made up of the Great Northern, the Northern Pacific, and the Burlington.

While financiers, speculators, and railroad men from Cornelius Vanderbilt to Hill and Harriman were assembling these giant rail units, similar activities by similar men were building up and consolidating wealth and economic power in other enterprises, such as steel and oil.

8

Men of Steel

The Robber Barons of the railroads could not have prospered as they did without the iron and steel industry, both in the United States and abroad, to supply them with materials, chiefly rails. The iron and steel industry, in turn, could not have prospered as it did had not the nation been intent on putting together a continental network of railroad tracks. And the Robber Baron of iron and steel who prospered the most was Andrew Carnegie (1835–1919).

For about fifty years after the Civil War, half of all the iron and steel produced in the United States was used by the railroads in one form or another: rails, bridges, and rolling stock. At the start of this period, large quantities of rails were imported from Great Britain, but as time went on the high tariff on imported rails and American advances in technology and productivity secured most of the market for such men as Carnegie. The United States in 1860 produced 1 million tons of pig iron; by 1920 the figure was 36 million tons. In 1875, 795,000 tons of iron and steel rails were manufactured in America, and production reached a peak of nearly 1.1 million tons in 1882, when railroad building was at its height.

Andrew Carnegie, who by the late nineteenth century was producing more of this iron and steel than anyone else, was born on November 25, 1835, in Dunfermline, Scotland. His father was a weaver, working in the family's cottage at a time when the factory system was about to doom the manufacturing of textiles in the home. Dunfermline was a hotbed of radical politics— meaning in those days agitation for the secret ballot, universal male suffrage, and other such democratic advances. Carnegie's father was an active radical and the boy soon picked up a fervor for political democracy that he never lost. He attended school in the village until 1848 when the family emigrated to the United States. This was done chiefly at his mother's urging, for she was more energetic and farsighted than her husband and saw that the cottage weaving industry was declining.

The family settled in Pittsburgh, Pennsylvania, and Andrew found a job as a bobbin boy in a textile factory at $1.20 a week. Only in his thirteenth year, he had to be at the factory before daylight and work until after dark, with only a short lunch period. Before long he was offered a job at $2 a week in another factory where he was assigned to keeping the steam engine, located in the basement, in running condition, a lonely and frightening task for the boy. In the spring of 1849, when he heard that a job as a messenger boy in a Pittsburgh telegraph office was available at $2.50 a week, he applied and was hired. Quick, energetic, and with a pleasing personality, Andrew not only became head messenger but within three years had also learned to be a telegraph operator and was earning the satisfactory, for those days, sum of $20 a month. He was able to help his parents buy a house. For recreation, Andrew organized a debating society and read widely in the books of a library for young working men.

When Thomas A. Scott, then superintendent of the western division of the Pennsylvania Railroad, decided to install his own telegraph in his office, his eye fell on Carnegie. Scott offered him the job of operator at $35 a month and Carnegie took it. This was one of the turning points of his life, at the age of seventeen. Carnegie soon became Scott's right-hand man rather than just his telegraph operator and learned thoroughly the railroad business. On one occasion, when Scott was absent, a serious accident tied up traffic on the Pennsylvania. With little hesitation, Carnegie issued orders in Scott's name and straightened out matters. When Scott became vice-president of the road in 1859, he named Carnegie superintendent of the western division at the age of twenty-four.

At the outbreak of the Civil War in 1861, Scott was called to Washington to help organize the railroads to serve the Union Army. Scott asked Carnegie to join him, and the latter entered Washington in the cab of a locomotive pulling a train that brought a Massachusetts regiment to help defend the capital. Carnegie repaired a telegraph line on the way. When the first major engagement, the Battle of Bull Run, was fought, Carnegie was at a telegraph station five miles from the battlefield. He suffered a slight sunstroke in the course of the day and ever after dreaded extreme heat. Carnegie saw quite a bit of President Lincoln at the War Department and wrote in his autobiography: "He was the most perfect democrat."

Carnegie returned to Pittsburgh and his job with the Pennsylvania in September 1861. He hated war in general but was very patriotic, strongly antislavery, and believed the South had no right to secede. Nevertheless, he did not volunteer, feeling his service in Washington and his work with the Pennsylvania were valuable contributions to the cause. When he was drafted in 1864, he paid a substitute, a recent Irish immigrant, $850 to serve in his place, as the Conscription Act of 1863 allowed.

Carnegie took his first step toward becoming a capitalist and a wealthy man in 1856 when, at Scott's suggestion, he bought a few shares of Adams Express. He borrowed $600 from Scott to make the purchase. When he received his first dividend check—for $10—he exclaimed: "Here's the goose that lays the golden eggs." In 1859, when Carnegie's salary from the Pennsylvania was $1,500 a year, he invested in the Woodruff Sleeping Car Company, his connection with it having come about when the inventor sold his idea to the railroad. Carnegie borrowed $217.50 from a bank to make an initial payment but the company was so successful that dividends easily took care of future payments and within two years his annual income from the investment was $5,000. Carnegie was instrumental in 1868 in arranging a merger between this company and what became the Pullman Palace Car Company. He and Scott came out of the deal with nearly a quarter of the shares in the new company, but Carnegie sold out his interest during the Panic of 1873.

In 1861, only two years following the drilling of the first well, Carnegie and some others invested $40,000 in oil production after an inspection trip to the Pennsylvania oil fields, north of Pittsburgh. Eventually, they profited to the extent of $5 million from this one small investment. With his growing interests in several fields keeping him busy, Carnegie left the Pennsylvania Railroad in March 1865. He and some others organized a telegraph company in 1867, merged it with another, which produced a large profit, and then in 1874 sold out to the largest company in the field, Western Union, at a further profit. Through his railroad connections, Carnegie was asked to act as agent for the sale of American bonds in London and between 1867 and 1873 disposed of about $30 million worth, receiving a commission on the sales.

By the end of 1868 Carnegie was worth $400,000 and had an income of $56,110 that year. He was thirty-three years old, and wrote a note to himself that he should not try to increase his fortune, but spend any surplus on philanthropies each year and "cast aside business forever." Moreover, he told himself he should settle in Oxford, England, study for three years, "get a thorough education" and make the acquaintance of "literary men." Finally, he warned himself: "Whatever I engage in I must push inordinately therefor [sic] should I be careful to choose that life which will be the most elevating in character."

Carnegie did not take his own advice and, in fact, was already involved in one aspect of the iron and steel industry. In 1862 he had invested in a company organized to make iron bridges and in 1865 this firm was reorganized on a larger scale. Here, as usual, Carnegie was looking into the future. Not only were railroads providing a market for many more bridges than ever, but they needed iron, rather than wood, to support the heavier rails and rolling stock and to rid themselves of the damaging fires that regularly destroyed wooden bridges. Carnegie was not satisfied with the operations of the mill that made the iron for the bridge company and in a short while combined it with another as Carnegie, Klopman and Company, of which he held the controlling interest. He was now fully launched on the career that was to be his main concern until the turn of the century.

Among his associates were his brother, Thomas Carnegie (1843–86), and Henry Phipps (1839–1930). The brothers looked much alike, but Thomas was more cautious, quiet but with a lively wit. Phipps, born in Philadelphia, moved to Pittsburgh in 1845 and was later a next door neighbor of the Carnegies. Mrs. Carnegie sewed shoes at home for Phipp's father, who was a master shoemaker. Phipps held various jobs before buying an interest in a scale manufacturing business in 1861. He became a partner of Carnegie in 1867 and was associated with him from then on. Phipps was much like Thomas Carnegie and helped the growing iron business steer a sane financial course. He retired in 1901 with a sizable fortune.

A great change in the iron and steel business was in process in the early 1870's. The Bessemer method for making steel was discovered independently in 1856 by Sir Henry Bessemer (1813–98) in Great Britain, and by William Kelly (1811–88), an American. The principle of the process is the oxidation of impurities in iron by blowing air through the iron when it is molten. Such steel is much harder and more durable than iron. Steel rails last much longer than iron ones and steel of this kind made the construction of tall buildings possible.

Returning from England in 1872, where he met Bessemer, Carnegie was resolved to build a steel plant using the new process and to devote his efforts to producing and selling steel. A new company was organized in November 1872 and construction of a plant near Pittsburgh began. Work continued in spite of the financial panic of the next year, and the depression made it possible to buy at lower prices materials needed to build the plant. The plant, the Edgar Thomson Steel Works, named for the man who was president of the Pennsylvania when Carnegie went to work for it, began production in August 1875. When Carnegie entered the field, only 94,000 tons of Bessemer steel a year were being produced in the United States. By 1880, the annual figure was 954,000 tons, a ten-fold increase, and Carnegie produced more of it than any other company.

After iron ore, the most essential material in the production of steel is coke, for smelting the ore, and consequently the Carnegie company had to be assured of a large supply. It found its primary supplier in Henry Clay Frick (1849–1919). Frick was born December 19, 1849, near Pittsburgh. Polite and studious in school, he did well in mathematics and began his business career by taking a clerking job in an uncle's store in 1863. Five years later he went to work in a store in Pittsburgh, where he advanced rapidly, then took the position of chief bookkeeper in his grandfather's prosperous distillery.

In 1871, when he was twenty-two, Frick became interested in the coke industry through a cousin and joined in forming the Frick Coke Company. At the time there seemed to be an oversupply of coke, but Frick plunged in, borrowing money and resolved to add to the 300 acres and 50 ovens he started with. A year later he had 100 more acres of excellent coal land and had erected 150 more ovens. Furthermore, he was selling all the coke he could produce. As steel production climbed, especially in the Carnegie mills, the price of coke rose. In December 1879, on his thirtieth birthday, Frick's books showed that he was worth a million dollars and so he had thereby achieved a boyhood ambition. He had nearly 1,000 employees, was shipping nearly 100 carloads of coke a day, and controlled about 80 percent of the area's production.

Frick caught Carnegie's shrewd eye and in 1881 the latter arranged to go into partnership in the coke company, which was reorganized. Within two years Carnegie and his associates owned half the coke company and so assured themselves of the supply of coke that was essential to them. By 1887, the number of coke ovens increased to 5,000 and 6,000 tons per day were produced. That same year the coke workmen struck and considerable violence ensued. Frick was all for fighting the workmen to the end, but the Carnegie interests, anxious that the coke supply not be interrupted, insisted on giving in to the men's demands. Frick resigned the presidency in anger, but in January 1888 the two sides made up and Frick resumed office. The joining of the Carnegie-Frick interests became complete in 1889 when Carnegie agreed to sell Frick 2 percent of the capital of Carnegie Brothers. Frick did not have to put up a cent as the share was to be paid for by dividends earned. He was also named chairman of the steel company and his share was later increased to 11 percent. Carnegie's judgment of Frick was vindicated. Frick acquired within a year the Duquesne Steel works, reorganized the management of the Carnegie plants, and worked effectively to keep costs down, a subject dear to Carnegie's heart. In 1890, the second year of Frick's management, the profit of the Carnegie steel plants was $5.35 million, an increase of $1.8 million over the previous year.

The Carnegie steel organization was never a corporation with stock available on the open market. Carnegie disliked intensely speculation in stocks, especially his own. The organization, under different names at different times, was a partnership and by agreement, if a partner retired or died, his interest was purchased by the partnership. Carnegie and his associates kept the lead in the steel industry by regularly installing new and more efficient machinery and by taking advantage of new technological processes. They also from time to time acquired plants others had built. Such a purchase in 1883 brought them the Homestead works. This plant, in the Pittsburgh area, was started by another group of steel men who found themselves continually plagued by labor troubles and within two years were happy to sell out to the Carnegie interests.

Occasionally Carnegie entered into agreements—pools—with other steel producers to limit production, but usually he preferred to play a lone hand. He sought high production and low costs, which made it possible for him to undersell others and still show a profit. The Thomson works, for example, made a profit of $1.25 million a year between 1881 and 1886 and Carnegie insisted that most of this be put back into plant improvement and expansion. Some of his partners would have preferred larger dividends. In 1892, all the operations were consolidated into the Carnegie Steel Company, Ltd., of which Carnegie held a 55.33 percent interest. Frick and Phipps each held 11 percent, and nineteen other partners 1 percent each, with the remainder held for younger men who might earn the right to be admitted to partnership. Carnegie by now controlled the largest steel company in the world.

Carnegie was a divided man in his approach to relations with the men who worked in his plants. From his Scottish and family background, he believed in equality and the rights of men to organize, and he said in a magazine article that "trades-unions upon the whole are beneficial both to labor and capital." He also liked to think that he was popular with the working men and that they would do as he wished if he treated them in a paternal manner. At the same time, Carnegie remained absolutely intent on keeping costs down and producing steel cheaper than anyone else. Part of this effort inevitably had to be attempts to hold down wage costs. In 1877, at the urging of the manager of the Thomson works, he accepted the institution of the eight-hour shift in place of the twelve-hour shift, seven days a week. When, however, no other steelmakers followed his example, he returned the plant to the longer shift on January 1, 1888. On this occasion he met with the workers and talked them into the longer day, with a profit-sharing sliding scale of wages, on the excuse that if the eight-hour day were continued, he would have to reduce wages.

At the Homestead plant the company had a contract with a union which was very powerful, even though it represented only eight hundred highly skilled workers out of the total of thirty-eight hundred men. The contract was to expire June 30, 1892, and Carnegie, before sailing for England in late April to spend several months abroad as usual, agreed with Frick that the end of the contract should be used as an occasion for getting rid of the union. The excuse was that the company did not have contracts with unions at any of its other plants. The company would also continue the sliding scale of wages and reduce the rates for those few men who were paid by tonnage production rather than by hourly rates. If the men refused these terms, Carnegie told Frick to close the plant.

Frick took a much harder line toward the men and the union than did Carnegie and prepared for a battle. He had a strong stockade built around three sides of the plant, and running down to the river on each side of the piers. The fence had holes in it suitable for rifle barrels and there was barbed wire on top. He also arranged with the Pinkerton Detective Agency to send three hundred armed guards should they be needed. The strike began and Frick asked to have the Pinkertons arrive on the morning of July 6. When their two barges approached the plant's piers, they were met with rifle fire from the enraged strikers and one guard was killed and eleven injured. After suffering in the heat until late afternoon, the guards surrendered. The leaders of the strike promised them safe passage through town if they gave up their arms, which they did, but the leaders were unable to make good on their guarantee. The men and women of Homestead attacked with any weapon available, including umbrellas and stockings filled with scrap iron. Three more Pinkertons were killed and every one of them injured in one of the nation's bloodiest labor battles.

The riot brought to Homestead eight thousand troops of the Pennsylvania militia to restore order, and Frick began to hire new workers, informing the old ones that if they did not apply by July 21 they would be out of a job. Homestead reopened with seven hundred strikebreakers and the strike, for practical purposes, was over. But the violence was not. On July 23 a man by the name of Alexander Berkman (1870?–1936) made his way into Frick's office and shot him twice with a pistol. Bleeding profusely, Frick helped subdue his assailant, then sat quietly while a doctor extracted the two bullets. He also insisted on finishing some work before he would allow himself to be taken home, where he recovered. Berkman, politically an anarchist, was born in Russian Poland and brought to the United States about 1877. He served fourteen years in jail for the assault.

Public opinion and much editorial opinion in newspapers, both in the United States and in Great Britain, were on the side of the strikers because of the use of the hated Pinkerton guards. Carnegie, who had not intervened, was harshly condemned for letting matters get to such a stage, especially in view of his often stated sympathy for labor, which he now seemed to have abruptly abandoned. He and Frick and the steel company were even blamed in some quarters for the defeat in November of the Republican candidate for president, Benjamin Harrison, by Grover Cleveland. If he had been on hand, Carnegie probably would not have built the stockade or hired the Pinkertons but would simply have closed the plant while the strikers thought matters over. Frick was much more of a despot who consistently wanted to crush any strike with whatever force was necessary.

The depression that began in 1893 reduced the Carnegie company's profits, but they were still considerable. Wages were cut that year and again in 1895, but some improvement in business brought bonuses for the workmen. Unlike other steelmakers, Carnegie as usual kept his mills running during the depression and so kept the men at work. Also, he took advantage of low prices to modernize the plants.

Another concern of the steelmaster was the securing of a

steady and large source of iron ore to meet the ever growing demands of the mills. At this time, the Mesabi Range, stretching one hundred twenty miles across north central Minnesota, was beginning to be recognized for what it was: the most valuable iron ore deposit on the North American continent. When an opportunity to invest in it was first presented to Frick, he was strongly in favor, but Carnegie was not, although he changed his mind. Then in 1894 John D. Rockefeller, looking for some place to invest some of the millions he was making in the petroleum industry so that they would produce still more profits, bought a large interest in the Mesabi Range. Two years later, the Carnegie interests and Rockefeller reached an agreement whereby the former would pay the oilman a royalty of twenty-five cents a ton for the ore they took out and would ship it on Rockefeller-owned railroads and Great Lakes steamships. Although only thirty thousand tons of ore had been extracted in 1892, by 1901 the total was more than nine million tons. Even the busy Carnegie mills were assured of all the ore they could use.

Until the early 1890's, the Carnegie mills produced steel in billet form for use in making finished articles but, except for rails, had performed little of the final steps. Carnegie realized that the market for rails was a declining one since the rail system was reaching its limits. He also foresaw growing markets for structural steel, steel railroad cars, and many other products. In going into these lines, Carnegie would compete directly with other companies that now bought his raw steel, such as the manufacturers of wire and tinplate. He would move toward verticality, a completely integrated operation from raw materials to finished goods. This step would also help meet the greater competition of the 1890's caused by the fact that in recent years almost all the plants except Carnegie's had been amalgamated into about a dozen large firms. The financier J. P. Morgan was the moving spirit behind the mergers.

Carnegie waged another battle, in his effort to keep costs down, with the Pennsylvania Railroad. He felt, with some evidence to justify his feeling, that because of the railroad's monopolistic position in Pittsburgh, it was charging him higher freight rates than other steelmakers in areas where two or more railroads competed for the traffic. Although he got some concessions from the Pennsylvania in 1896 when he promised not to build his own road to the coke fields, he was resolved to have his own line between Pittsburgh and the Lake Erie port of Conneaut, Ohio. He, therefore, took over a ramshackle road and rebuilt it into a model of a freight line. In 1898 he bought all the land around Conneaut harbor and the following year acquired his own steamship line on the Great Lakes. Ore could now be brought from the Mesabi Range to Pittsburgh cheaply enough to satisfy even Carnegie.

Carnegie had never entirely forgotten his view of many years before to stop making money and devote himself to other pursuits, and so in 1898 he indicated he was willing to consider selling out his majority interest. Frick and Phipps set out to arrange a deal and informed Carnegie they had a group interested in buying the Carnegie steel empire. They were rather mysterious about it and when Carnegie found out that among the leaders of the syndicate were speculators whom he despised, the deal was called off. One typical member of the syndicate was John W. Gates (1855–1911), known as "Bet-a-Million Gates" because of his propensity for taking chances. He was said to have made $12 million speculating in stocks on Wall Street and also to have been wiped out in a grain speculation scheme in Chicago. He had, though, seen a prosperous future for the barbed wire business, set up a plant to manufacture it and, as merger followed merger, made millions. The climax of his efforts was reached in 1898 when the American Steel and Wire Company was formed with a capitalization of $90 million. Gates was indeed a colorful figure but he had no sense of public responsibility. Frick and Phipps had secured for Carnegie an option payment of $1.7 million when negotiations began and when the deal collapsed, Carnegie refused to return any of it, even though $170,000 had come out of his two partners' own pockets.

This unpleasant episode was but one more of a string of events that drove Carnegie and Frick apart. In 1899 they had a bitter disagreement over the price the Frick Coke Company was to charge the steel company for its product. The struggle came to an end in December when Frick resigned his position. There followed a further quarrel over how much he should receive for his interest in the steel and coke companies and a lawsuit was threatened. Finally, an agreement was reached under which Frick got a little more than $31 million in stocks and bonds. He and Carnegie never saw each other again. That same year, 1899, the steel company's profits reached a new high of $20 million, and in the following year Carnegie produced nearly half of the ten million tons of steel to come out of American mills.

In retirement, Frick devoted his time to his investments and to art collecting. He had once linked the two by calling railroads "the Rembrandts of investment." Following this opinion, Frick became the largest individual owner of railroad stock in the world, holding more than $40 million worth at one time. He spent about the same number of dollars assembling a collection of more than one hundred paintings, most of them acknowledged master-pieces. He housed the collection in the mansion he had built on upper Fifth Avenue in New York at a cost of $5,400,000. At his death the house and the works of art became a museum open to the public. Frick was a handsome man, of medium height, with a strong jaw, who always appeared to be calm and decisive. He took up a few hobbies, such as fast motoring and golf, but his attitude toward life was expressed simply as "work and sleep."

The steel industry in 1900 appeared headed for a period of bitter competition if Carnegie went ahead with his plans for producing a greater variety of steel goods. The men who saw themselves threatened turned to Morgan in the hope that he could arrange further mergers or some sort of truce in the industry. The first change in the situation came as a result of a quiet, private dinner in New York on December 12, 1900. The two men who arranged the dinner invited both Morgan and Charles M. Schwab (1862–1939), now president of Carnegie's company. Schwab, a genial, outgoing person, began his career in a dollar a day job in the mill. At twenty-five he was put in charge of the Homestead works, then became general superintendent of the Thomson works. After the devastating Homestead strike in 1892, he was again put in charge there and succeeded in restoring calm and peace. By the turn of the century, Schwab was Carnegie's right-hand man and the two had a father and son relationship.

Schwab spoke at the December dinner, presenting an enthusiastic account of the future of the American steel industry

as the world's leader. After the dinner Morgan drew Schwab
aside, talked for a bit and arranged for a longer conversation early
in January. Carnegie knew nothing of this discussion but when
Schwab told him the story and indicated that Morgan was
prepared to buy the Carnegie company, the steelmaster, after
some hesitation, agreed to consider the idea. He wrote down a
few figures on a piece of paper, indicating he wanted
$480,000,000 for his company. Schwab took the paper to Morgan
who looked at it and said: "I accept this price." The result was the
formal organization on March 3, 1901, of the United States Steel
Corporation, combining the Carnegie plants with others. The
new firm manufactured 60 percent of all the iron and steel
produced in the country, owned 1,000 miles of railroads, 112 ore
vessels, and coal fields with 700 million tons of coal available.
Schwab, only thirty-nine, became the first president of the
company. The new and largest commercial enterprise in the
world was capitalized at $1 billion, a good deal of which rep-
resented "good will," or was watered stock, depending on one's
point of view. Carnegie, for his part, received 5 percent bonds with
a par value of $225,639,000. He had a vault especially constructed
in Hoboken, New Jersey, to keep the bonds safe.

After selling out, Carnegie devoted much of his time to
giving away most of his fortune and went about it with the same
energy and practicality that had made him rich. He did not want
to give his money to the usual kind of charities; he wanted to use it
where it would do away with the causes of misery and ignorance.
His philanthropy that touched the most people directly was the
2,811 free public libraries given at a cost of more than $50 million.
Carnegie donated the building but only if a town or city agreed to
stock it with books and operate it. Not forgetting his native land,
Carnegie set up a Scottish Universities Trust with a gift of $10
million and provided a park and other facilities for his birthplace,
Dunfermline. Churches received 7,689 organs from him at a cost
of over $6 million. He donated $17 million to several hundred
colleges and universities, selecting small ones rather than the
best known institutions. One time, after a tour of the Princeton
campus, when many hints were dropped as to the need for such
things as library facilities and science laboratories, Carnegie
instead gave $400,000 to build a lake. He hated football and

hoped having a place to row would take the students' minds off the rough game.

His money founded the Carnegie Institute of Technology, in Pittsburgh, and the Carnegie Institution of Washington. At the same time he maintained a private pension fund that paid out a quarter of a million dollars a year to individuals. One of his major philanthropies was the establishment of the Carnegie Teachers Pension Fund, endowed with $10 million, whose name was soon changed to the Carnegie Foundation for the Advancement of Teaching. One of Carnegie's constant dreams had been that he might be instrumental in bringing about international peace, so in 1903 he agreed to give $1.5 million to build at The Hague a building for the Permanent Court of Arbitration. He thought of it as a "temple of peace," but to his dismay it became known as the "Peace Palace." He also, in 1910, set up the Carnegie Endowment for International Peace with a gift of $10 million.

Carnegie's largest philanthropy and the one that has exerted more influence than any other was the Carnegie Corporation of New York, which he established in 1911 "to promote the advancement and diffusion of knowledge." He gave it $125 million, far more than any individual had ever before given to a single cause. Even so, when he was seventy-six-years old he found he still had $150 million of the United States Steel Corporation bonds left. As he wrote to his fellow millionaire-philanthropist John D. Rockefeller, Sr., "The way of the philanthropist is hard." Later in his life, when he asked an aide how much he had given away in all, he was told the total was $324,657,399. "Wherever did I get all that money?" Carnegie wondered.

Andrew Carnegie was more articulate and, apparently, more concerned than any other Robber Baron about the problems being created by modern industrialism and by the accumulation of extraordinarily large fortunes. He wrote many magazine articles and, besides his autobiography, published two books growing out of his business experience: *Triumphant Democracy* and *The Gospel of Wealth*. He was against privilege that came by birth and he was strongly democratic in political matters, but he was also a defender of capitalism and of private wealth. He was opposed to imperialism, but believed that Canada should become a part of the United States. He also foresaw a federation of the United States and the British Empire that would bring world peace. When the Spanish-American War broke out in 1898, Carnegie favored it because he felt Cuba should be freed and Spain driven from the Western Hemisphere. When, though, the United States retained the Philippine Islands at the end of the war, he was outraged. He actively campaigned against the treaty with Spain and even offered President McKinley, out of his own pocket, $20 million (the same amount the United States was going to give Spain) for the islands so he could set them free.

Carnegie remained a strong defender of the right to accumulate money, saying it would be a mistake to shoot the millionaires, "for they are the bees that make the most honey." He did, however, oppose the hoarding of millions and the passing on of fortunes to younger generations that had not earned them. "The man who dies thus rich, dies disgraced," he said, arguing that it was the duty of those who made fortunes to give them away while they lived for the benefit of others.

The steelmaster also showed more interest in intellectual matters than most of his contemporaries. This probably stemmed from his family background. He was a lifelong reader who, when he became important, cultivated authors such as Mark Twain, Matthew Arnold, and John Morley. He also was well acquainted with British statesmen such as the Earl of Rosebery and William Gladstone and did not hesitate to give them advice on political matters.

Carnegie did not marry until he was fifty-one and his wife was twenty-one years his junior. They had one daughter. Although the Carnegies lived well, they never spent money on themselves in any showy way. The mansion Carnegie built on upper Fifth Avenue cost $1.5 million and is now the Cooper-Hewitt Museum. His greatest luxury was Skibo Castle in northern Scotland, on an estate that eventually totaled thirty-two thousand acres. The castle was built of native stone, but the hidden framework was of steel made in his own mills in Pittsburgh. Andrew Carnegie was a small man, lively in both mind and body. He had a pinkish complexion and light blue eyes. Although he appeared vain and arrogant at times, he was usually charming and genial. He died on August 11, 1919, leaving only

$30 million of his once great fortune. His wife and daughter had been provided for earlier, so two-thirds of this residue went to the Carnegie Corporation.

"Put all your eggs in one basket," Carnegie once said, "and then watch that basket." He consistently followed that advice himself once he got thoroughly involved in the manufacture of iron and steel. Another man who followed this same principle and became even richer was John D. Rockefeller, Sr., the ruler of a new industry built on petroleum.

9
Flowing Gold

Railroad construction and operation, and the manufacture of iron and steel were established industries when the Robber Barons of the latter part of the nineteenth century made them into giant enterprises. The oil industry, on the other hand, did not exist until 1859, but it grew even faster than these older industries. Like the steel industry, it had a leader of Andrew Carnegie's stature in John D. Rockefeller, Sr. (1839–1937).

Oil, or petroleum, had been known for many years as a substance that seeped to the surface in certain places. Sometimes it ruined brine wells from which salt was procured. Known as Seneca oil or Indian oil it was reputed to have medicinal value and was bottled and sold for this purpose. There was, for example, "Kier's Petroleum or Rock Oil, celebrated for its wonderful curative powers." In 1855 two men were curious enough about oil to send a sample to Benjamin Silliman, Jr., professor of chemistry at Yale University, for examination. When he described to them its chemical properties they decided further action was worthwhile and engaged Edwin L. Drake, (1819–80), who conferred on himself the title of "colonel," to drill a well. In 1858 Drake went to Titusville, Pennsylvania, on Oil Creek in the northwestern part of the state, where oil was known to exist. He engaged a local brine-well driller called "Uncle Billy" Smith to do the work and, after considerable effort, oil was struck. The well was down to a depth of sixty-nine feet on August 17, 1859, when the first producing well in the United States began to flow at the rate of about twenty barrels a day.

In a short time the Titusville area resembled the California gold fields of ten years earlier as men rushed to acquire the riches promised by the black, flowing liquid. High prices were paid for land where oil might or might not be struck. Boom towns sprang up overnight and faded just as fast if no oil was found. As early as the year after Drake's discovery, two hundred thousand barrels of oil were pumped out of the ground. By reason of geographical location and the availability of transportation facilities, Cleveland, Ohio, became one of the first important centers of oil refining. Kerosene was the most valuable product distilled from the crude oil in these early days of the industry and it rapidly replaced whale oil and candles for illumination.

At this time an industrious young man in his early twenties was already on his way to modest prosperity as a partner in a produce business in Cleveland, where he could not help but be aware of the new and booming oil industry. John D. Rockefeller, Sr., was born at Richford in upstate New York on July 8, 1839. His father was a show-off and a wanderer who was away from home for months at a time, leaving John D.'s mother to take care of the family, although he provided them with adequate money. The father was a dealer in patent medicines and later in Cleveland listed himself as an "herb doctor." The family moved to Cleveland in 1853. There John D. went to high school, graduated in 1855, and that fall got a job as a clerk for a firm of commission merchants who dealt in grain and other commodities. From his salary of $3.50 a week, he gave 10 percent to the Baptist church to which he belonged.

By 1858 he was making $600 a year and had saved $800. With that and another $1,000 which he borrowed from his father at the high rate of 10 percent interest, he formed a commodity-dealing firm with a partner. The Civil War brought prosperity to the new company as prices went up. Later, Rockefeller claimed he wanted to enlist in the Union army but that so many people were dependent on the business, which would have to fold up if he left, that he had to stay home. He said he contributed a good deal of money to the Union cause.

As Rockefeller, who when a little younger had expressed a

determination to make $100,000, saw the prosperity of the refineries around him, he joined two other men, including his partner in the commodity business, in establishing an oil refinery. The refinery business was in its infancy and the refining process itself so simple that $10,000 was enough to start a small one. Rockefeller also was aware that the production end of the oil industry was an uncertain one and that prices of crude oil fluctuated widely. At the refinery end, however, profits were more stable and more certain. Once in the refinery business, Rockefeller wanted to expand rapidly whereas his partners were more conservative. As a result, he bought out one of them in 1865 and at twenty-six controlled his own refinery, which was the largest in Cleveland and which within a year had revenues of $1 million.

The business grew, and in 1870 it was reorganized as the Standard Oil Company of Ohio with a capital of $1 million. That same year the railroads running between the East Coast and the Midwest became involved in one of their regular rate wars. Standard Oil offered to the Lake Shore Railroad to guarantee the shipment of sixty carloads of oil every day if it was given a large rebate. The railroad agreed to charge a standard rate of only $1.65 per barrel for crude from the oil regions to Cleveland and then to New York in refined form, compared with the announced rate of $2.40 a barrel for the combined trip. The rate was to be secret, but the terms leaked out. Other refiners were angry but none of them could guarantee such large shipments. This was but the first of numerous occasions on which secret rebate agreements with railroads gave Standard Oil an advantage over smaller rivals.

During his first years in the oil business, Rockefeller was joined by two associates who were to be instrumental in making Standard Oil the giant it became. One of them was his brother William (1841–1922) and the other was Henry M. Flagler (1830–1913), a fellow commission merchant in Cleveland. William joined his brother's oil business in 1865 and after two years became the head of Standard Oil's exporting business in New York. Later, with some other executives of the company and some New York bankers, William became a part of the "Standard Oil Gang" that was notorious for speculating in stocks, particularly railroad and gas. Unlike his quiet, pious older brother, William was jovial and liked to live well. When he died he left all of his $150 million to $200 million fortune to his family with not a cent to charity.

Flagler, born in western New York State, brought some capital to the young oil company and became, after John D., the most powerful man in the organization. He took over the transportation problems and leased so many tank cars that other refiners found none were available. After a trip to Florida in 1883, Flagler became just as much interested in turning that state into a winter vacation spot, which he did almost single-handedly, as in oil. In 1886 he bought a struggling railroad and kept extending it so that by 1912 it reached Key West at the end of the southernmost string of United States islets. He created Palm Beach as a resort for the rich, with a luxury hotel there. Flagler also built hotels at other points along his railroad and it was said that wherever he built one he also built a church and a gambling house. He retired as a Standard Oil vice-president in 1908.

Between 1870 and 1872 Rockefeller made several moves toward taking over as many competitors as possible and he began to earn a reputation for sharp and ruthless dealings—a reputation that was to stay with him the rest of his life. At the instigation of Thomas A. Scott, now president of the Pennsylvania Railroad, a company was chartered in Pennsylvania called the South Improvement Company. It was a holding company whose charter allowed it to do almost anything. Scott's idea was to bring into the company the three main railroads that carried oil, together with the leading refiners. They would make an agreement on rates and on sharing the traffic that would be to their advantage and would squeeze out competitors. In early 1872 Standard Oil joined the group and agreed to the scheme, under which certain rates were announced publicly, while the members received a rebate from them. Standard was to pay ninety cents less a barrel than its competitors outside the group. Not only that but the South Improvement Company participants would also receive from the railroads a "drawback" on the freight rates their competitors paid; that is, for every barrel of oil another company shipped to Cleveland, Rockefeller's company received forty cents a barrel from the amount the other company paid the railroad. The arrangement was a very profitable one for the roads and Standard

Oil, but the producers in the oil regions of western Pennsylvania were left out. When word of the plan leaked, there was such a furor that the South Improvement Company decided it would be wise to go out of business.

Rockefeller, busy absorbing as many of his competitors as he could, aimed first at his largest Cleveland competitor which, like many others, was losing money. He convinced the owners to sell out to him in return for Standard Oil stock. Smaller refiners soon fell in line and by the end of 1872, Rockefeller had acquired thirty-four rivals, including almost every refinery in Cleveland. Standard Oil could refine ten thousand barrels of crude a day, half of all the oil produced at the time. But Rockefeller was by no means satisfied. He wanted to enlarge Standard Oil, to control the industry, and to bring order and efficiency into the refinery business, both for their own sake and so as to make more profits. In 1872 and early 1873 he acquired two large refineries in the New York City area and the next year a large one at Oil City in the heart of the oil regions. Before long, Standard owned most of the plants there, and by 1875 the Standard Oil flag flew over the largest refineries in the Philadelphia and Pittsburgh areas.

Rockefeller used his growing economic power in 1874 to arrange as unfair a freight rate system as was ever devised. The railroads agreed to charge Standard the same rate for shipping a barrel of crude from the oil regions to Cleveland or Pittsburgh, and for then transporting the finished product to New York, as they would charge for simply carrying a barrel of crude from the oil fields to New York or Philadelphia. One reason Standard sought this advantage was to get a larger share of the export market for oil products. By 1873 this market reached 5.5 million barrels, most of which was shipped out of the country from East Coast ports. Until 1873 Standard sold its products to independent wholesalers and other dealers, but Rockefeller did not like the idea of having no control over these middlemen who, among other activities, sometimes adulterated Standard's products. He was determined, therefore, to enter this part of the industry, too.

In his round of acquisitions in the early 1870's, Rockefeller found two more associates who helped Standard on the road to monopoly and who shared in the millions the company produced. They were Charles Pratt (1830–91) and Henry H. Rogers

(1840–1909), who were partners in a Brooklyn refinery when John D. bought it in 1874. Pratt was born in Massachusetts, went to work on a neighbor's farm when he was only ten, and moved to New York in 1851. He managed Standard affairs in Brooklyn, built a model tenement for his employees and founded Pratt Institute for artisans, designers, and draftsmen. Rogers was also born in Massachusetts and worked as a brakeman on a railroad before going to the oil regions with a friend. Each had about $600 and with that money they started a small refinery. Rogers devised the first machinery for separating naphtha from crude oil. When he joined Standard Oil he was placed in charge of all production matters and handled them ably. Like William Rockefeller, he used his oil fortune for speculation in other fields, such as copper. At one time he controlled transportation on Staten Island and also was the sole owner of a railroad worth $40 million. He became a friend of Mark Twain and straightened out the author's business affairs when Twain had gotten them into a tangle.

By the late 1870's, Standard Oil had no effective competition in the refinery field except for a little in the New York area. It refined just over 90 percent of all the oil products in the United States in 1878 and, two years later, the figure climbed to 95 percent. In the latter part of the 1870's Standard moved strongly into the wholesale field, setting up regional territories and very efficiently striving to eliminate competition. Standard's method was to cut prices, even if that action lost money for a while, until it drove any competition out of business. Then prices went back up. The company paid good wages but could be quite ruthless if there was any labor trouble. When barrel makers struck in 1877, Rockefeller hired three hundred special police and let them attack a crowd of strikers when they attempted to prevent strikebreakers from entering a plant. A wage cut was the cause of the strike, but that year Standard Oil paid a dividend of $80 for each $100 share of stock. About this time, someone estimated that John D. was receiving an average of $720 an hour in dividends.

When he became forty in 1879, Rockefeller was the unchallenged head of the largest industrial organization in the country. The Standard Oil Company held a practical monopoly in its field, and it had achieved this without any government privilege, any patent, or exclusive control of raw materials. The company was worth $70 million and Rockefeller's share was $13 million. He probably was worth as much again in other investments. The Rockefellers, though, continued to live on a comparatively modest scale and the father did not let his children feel they were rich.

From the start of his career in oil, Rockefeller had kept out of the production end for the most part. Too many small producers operated wells, they often pumped more oil than the market could use, and they were never able to organize for their own protection. It was safer and cheaper for Standard Oil, with its immense purchasing power, to buy the crude oil it needed. However, as it worked toward a monopoly of refining, it also endeavored to secure control over transportation, both of crude and of refined products. Rockefeller made deals with the railroads and played them off against each other, but the building of pipelines to carry oil presented a new problem and a new opportunity. At first they were short lines intended only to carry crude from the wells to the nearest railhead. Gradually they were extended and competed with the railroads, which in turn sought control of them. Rockefeller took steps to prevent the railroads from securing a pipeline monopoly by entering the field himself in 1873. By 1876 Standard owned four hundred miles of lines.

The Pennsylvania Railroad in 1877 decided to compete head-on with Standard, not only by owning pipelines but, through a subsidiary, by also entering the refinery business. Rockefeller, as usual, struck back promptly. He cut the price of kerosene, prevailed on the Erie and New York Central railroads to reduce their rates, and hastily built six hundred new tank cars. The battle between Rockefeller and Scott might have gone on for some time, but the nationwide rail strike of 1877 did so much damage to the Pennsylvania's financial position that it gave in and sold its pipeline to Standard Oil for a little more than a million dollars. By late 1877 Rockefeller controlled the existing pipelines as firmly as he did refining, but in 1879 the producers in the oil regions of Pennsylvania decided to give battle. The Tidewater Pipe Line Company constructed a 110-mile line to carry crude directly from the fields to refineries on the East Coast. This made allies again of Rockefeller and the railroads. Freight rates were

reduced, some independent refineries in the East were purchased to reduce the opponents' market for their crude, and
Standard Oil began building more pipelines of its own to connect
the fields to Cleveland and New York. The Tidewater Company
ran into financial difficulties and in 1883 reached an agreement
with Standard Oil whereby it would carry a little more than 10
percent of the crude eastward, leaving the rest to Rockefeller. By
this time, Standard owned about twelve thousand miles of
pipelines.

Although Rockefeller and his associates had a practical
monopoly of the oil industry, they were not satisfied with the
corporate and legal arrangements that governed the far-flung and
complicated organization. Under the law, the Standard Oil
Company of Ohio could not own stock in other companies or
operate in other states. Thus, plants which it in reality owned in
New York, for example, could not openly operate as part of the
Standard Oil Company. This problem was solved in 1882 by the
formation of a trust. Under its terms, the stockholders set up a
board of trustees to whom was turned over the stocks of the parent
company and of all subsidiary and allied companies. The stockholders in return received stock certificates and gave the nine
trustees (who included the Rockefeller brothers, Flagler, and
Pratt) authority to operate all facilities as they wished. The trust
was capitalized at $70 million, none of which was "water," and by
1890 its assets stood at more than $115 million and its earnings
were over $19 million. Almost two-sevenths of all the trust
certificates belonged to John D. The public did not realize it, but
he was now one of the richest men in America. For that matter,
the public did not even know the trust existed until 1888.

Behind the idea of the trust, which was later copied in other
fields such as sugar manufacturing and tobacco processing, was
the legal brain of Samuel C. T. Dodd (1836–1907), a lawyer who
was born in western Pennsylvania, the son of a carpenter. Earlier
in his career he had been on the opposing side, having denounced
the South Improvement Company and having represented the oil
producers against Standard Oil. Once he went to work for
Rockefeller, however, he was one of his most valuable assets.
Later, when the trust was outlawed he devised the holding
company plan for Rockefeller. Dodd unsuccessfully fought the

passage of the Sherman Antitrust Act, but later he convinced the Supreme Court that the law applied to combinations in restraint of trade only if they were "unreasonable."

The Standard Oil Company continued to grow and prosper during the 1880's and 1890's. This was due in part to its monopolistic position, partly to its superbly efficient operations, partly to the growth of the nation and, finally, to the invention of new machines and processes. Standard in 1883 owned more than thirty companies which operated forty refineries. It was producing a more varied line of products than originally: gasoline, lubricants, vaseline, and paraffin, for example. Rockefeller could boast that 95 percent of the railroad mileage in the country used Standard's lubricating oils. Better stoves were designed to use its oil products, but the really promising new development late in the century was the appearance of the internal combustion engine, requiring gasoline. By 1900, 18,500 such engines were manufactured during the year. When Henry Ford operated his first car, a Standard salesman sold him a can of oil. Standard became steadily more self-sufficient by producing its own equipment and materials, such as barrels, and in the five-year period from 1894 to 1898 made 223 million tin cans. All this time, the company also kept up its practice of fighting competition through an efficient and ruthless marketing organization.

Standard Oil went after the export market as competitively as it did the domestic one. In the 1870's the United States was the only oil supplier to Europe and Asia, but in the 1880's Russian oil entered the market and in the next decade oil began to come from Burma and the Dutch East Indies. In spite of this competition, American exports, chiefly from Standard Oil, increased regularly, reaching 740 million gallons in 1900. Standard established foreign marketing agencies in various countries and its products penetrated far into the interior of China, among other exotic places. With its usual tactics of price-cutting and espionage, Standard became as unpopular abroad as it was at home.

The company also continued to have difficulties with the legal aspects of the organization. Both the New York State Senate and a committee of the House of Representatives investigated trusts in 1888 and Rockefeller was called to testify. He was mild and deliberate, denied Standard Oil was a monopoly, denied it received lower railroad rates than competitors, and suffered losses of memory when certain questions were asked. In 1890 the state of Ohio brought suit against the Standard Oil Company on the grounds that it was violating the law by allowing its affairs to be controlled by the trust, made up largely of non-residents of Ohio. Two years later the court agreed and ordered the company to disassociate itself from the trust.

This action and the passage by Congress of the Sherman Antitrust Act caused the trustees, with the assistance of their counsel, Dodd, to look for a new way to protect their extremely valuable property. They found it in a New Jersey law, not common at that time, that permitted the formation of companies whose sole purpose was to hold the stock of other companies. The Standard Oil (New Jersey) Company was formed in June 1899 to exchange its stock for the certificates of the Standard Oil Trust and for the stock of twenty other companies involved. Capitalization was increased to $110 million. The legal arrangement was new but the same small group of men continued to manage the whole enterprise as they had under other forms of organization. The assets of Standard Oil in 1900 were $205 million and went up to $360 million in six years, at which time earnings were more than $83 million a year.

Formation of the holding company did not, however, solve all of Standard's problems. In the early years of the twentieth century a number of state and federal suits were begun against it. The most spectacular of these came to a climax in 1907 when the presiding federal judge, Kenesaw Mountain Landis, by name, found Standard Oil guilty and levied a fine of more than $29 million, the largest in history. It was, though, overturned on appeal and so Rockefeller never had to pay. The federal government launched another suit in November 1906, charging Standard Oil with violating the Sherman Act. After nearly fifteen thousand pages of testimony accumulated, the court found Standard guilty. The company, of course, appealed but at last, in March 1911, the Supreme Court upheld the conviction and ordered the company dissolved. Reading the decision, Chief Justice Edward D. White said that "the very genius for commercial organization soon begot an intent and purpose to exclude others." The company was given thirty days to dissolve itself. This was no small task, but the shares in the holding company were divided into shares in thirty-four operating companies and distributed. Rockefeller's shares were worth $160 million. The various Standard Oil stocks, now publicly traded on the exchange, went up in value by $200 million within a few months. In the meantime, the same small group of men, from an office in New York, continued to see to it that the many Standard companies worked together as one as they had before.

By this time Rockefeller was no longer active in the management of the oil empire, although he retained his holdings and his influence. He had gradually given up day-to-day participation and by 1897 was, in effect, retired. Nevertheless, he had many business interests to keep him occupied. His fortune amounted to about $200 million by then, and Rockefeller regularly sought profitable investments in other fields for the income that flowed from Standard Oil. He had substantial interests in sixteen railroads, nine mining companies, and several banks. His most profitable investment was his gradual acquisition of much of the Mesabi Range with its iron ore, beginning in 1893, when his fortune made it possible for him to take over the interests there of others who were ruined by the depression that began that year. As noted in the previous chapter, Rockefeller a few years later made a profitable leasing arrangement with Carnegie to use the ore.

The elder Rockefeller's chief assistants in the business affairs and in the philanthropy of his later years were his son, John D., Jr. (1874–1960) and a Baptist clergyman, Frederic T. Gates (1853–1929). The younger Rockefeller began participating in both the oil and the family business after he graduated from college, and he gradually took over more and more responsibility as he won his father's confidence. Gates first came to the elder Rockefeller's attention as a fund raiser for Baptist causes in which he was interested. Before long, Gates was working full time for Rockefeller, not only overseeing philanthropic activities but also managing many of the family's investments. Gates was an unusually able organizer and manager and was instrumental, for example, in carrying on the negotiations that ended in Rockefeller's control of the Mesabi Range ore.

That the Rockefellers had the same harsh attitude toward

labor as Henry Clay Frick and most of the other Robber Barons was demonstrated in 1913 during a strike at the Colorado Fuel and Iron Company workings in Colorado. At Gates's urging, the elder Rockefeller had acquired a controlling interest in 1907. Typical of mining towns of the time, wages were low, the workers got their pay in scrip which could be spent only in the company-owned store where prices were high, and the company owned the dismal houses in which the miners lived. In September 1913, nine thousand miners and their families went on strike, moved out of the company town, and set up tent camps, one of which they called Ludlow. They were harassed by hired security guards, and later the governor sent in the militia, most of whom became antagonistic toward the workers. On April 20, 1914, shooting broke out and the militia poured heavy fire into Ludlow. By the end of the day, forty people were dead, including women and children, and many more wounded.

When the mine operators refused an offer of federal mediation, a House committee held a hearing at which John D., Jr., was called to testify. He upheld what the owners and managers had done and refused to admit any blame or to consider recognizing a union. His father showed his approval by giving his son ten thousand shares of stock in the company. The public outcry against the Rockefellers was worse than any previous display of disapproval and, after a while, the younger Rockefeller realized times had changed and that something had to be done. In September 1915 he visited the area and met and talked with the miners and their families. The result was the so-called Rockefeller Plan whereby the miners by secret ballot elected representatives to a joint committee with management which would decide on working and living conditions, housing, education, and other matters.

Over the years John D., Sr., gave large amounts of money to Baptist groups, especially to help that denomination organize the University of Chicago in 1891. He contributed $10 million then and continued to give thereafter. When he appeared on campus in 1896 the students cheered him with: "John D. Rockefeller, wonderful man is he, / Gives all his spare change to the U. of C."

His money did not receive so warm a welcome, though, when he gave $100,000 to the Congregational Church for mis-

sionary work in 1905. A number of clergymen and others pro-
tested acceptance of the gift; one of the leading clergymen of the
day, the Reverend Washington Gladden, called it "tainted
money." This was at a time when Standard Oil was under regular
attacks in the courts and the press, but when it was admitted that
the Congregationalists had solicited the gift from Rockefeller, the
furor died down. This incident again demonstrated that Rockefeller was attacked for his wealth far more than others, such as
Carnegie or Morgan, but his fortune was just as honestly come by
as those of other Robber Barons, and more so than some. That
same year, 1905, he told a reporter that "God gave me my
money." By then he had come to believe that this was true, so
long as he used the money for the benefit of others.

Like Carnegie, Rockefeller did not give away many large
sums nor devote much time to philanthropy until his retirement
from day-to-day business affairs. With Gates at his side, Rockefeller began in 1901 to establish the philanthropic institutions that
made him the equal of Carnegie in giving. In 1901 he established
the Rockefeller Institute for Medical Research (now Rockefeller
University) and gave it $1.2 million in its first year. The General
Education Board was formed in 1903 with Gates as president and
it received $150 million in all. Rockefeller decided in 1910 to
establish his largest philanthropic organization, the Rockefeller
Foundation, but sentiment against him and Standard Oil was
such (the antitrust case was then before the Supreme Court) that
Congress refused to grant a charter. The Foundation in 1913
settled for a charter from New York State, and Rockefeller
endowed it with $100 million in its first two years. In all, he gave
to these three institutions and to the Laura Spelman Rockefeller
Memorial Foundation almost $447 million.

John D. Rockefeller, Sr., looked and acted more like a
conscientious bookkeeper than one of the half dozen most
powerful men in the United States. His face was narrow, usually
expressionless and he seemed detached to the point of coldness.
He was gentle and warm in his family circle, but his outward
manner did much to make the public dislike him. Although his
homes in Cleveland and New York, to which he moved in 1884,
and his later estate of Pocantico were large and expensive,
Rockefeller never flaunted his wealth as did some of the new

millionaires of the Gilded Age. Nor did he let his children show off. They walked to school instead of being escorted or chauffeured as were certain others.

Rockefeller's health was not good in the 1890's, presumably from his single-minded devotion to business, and a nervous disease in 1893 caused the loss of all his hair. Moreover, until he began spending most of his time at the Pocantico estate, near Tarrytown, New York, which eventually reached an extent of thirty-five hundred acres, he enjoyed little in the way of recreation. After he took up golf in 1899, he became so enthusiastic about it that he played every day on his own course on the estate. When necessary he had it cleared of snow. In the early years of the twentieth century, with the aid of a master of public relations, Ivy Lee, the public attitude toward Rockefeller began to change. He was seen as a unique American phenomenon and a slightly odd, benign, and very old man who gave away thirty thousand dimes one at a time to strangers who crossed his path. No one seems to know for sure whether or not Rockefeller's fortune ever passed the magic billion-dollar mark, but it certainly came close. By the time he died on May 23, 1937, in the ninety-eighth year of his life, he had transferred to John D., Jr., nearly half a billion dollars and his total philanthropic gifts totaled about the same sum. He had only $26.5 million in his possession by then, about the same as Carnegie possessed at his death.

As one of the most successful business men in history, Rockefeller, it was assumed, enjoyed all that amassing power and fortune entailed. Yet after forty years in the oil business he claimed it was all "work by day and worry by night. If I had foreseen the future I doubt whether I would have had the courage to go on." His known attention to details, among other habits, makes it hard to believe such a statement. On one occasion he went carefully over a report on the number of barrel bungs used in one refinery for the month and demanded to know what had become of seven hundred fifty of them not accounted for in the report. Another time he watched tops being soldered on tin cans after they were filled with Standard Oil products and asked how many drops of solder were used. On being told forty, he ordered a test using only thirty-nine drops. The test was successful and thereafter one drop of solder was saved on every can.

He was also presumed to be a monster who stopped at nothing to crush a competitor. One of the favorite anti-Rockefeller stories concerned the widow of a man who had owned a small refinery. The oil magnate supposedly offered her much less than the refinery was worth when she was forced to sell, but those who have examined all the evidence say the widow's story was incorrect. It was another example of the willingness of the public to believe the worst about Rockefeller. There were, though, many other instances in which the tactics of Standard Oil were less than honorable. Rockefeller was possessed with the idea that Standard Oil must be the only company in the business.

Two books were especially damaging to the public reputation of Rockefeller and Standard Oil. The first was *Wealth Against Commonwealth* by Henry Demarest Lloyd, published in 1894. It was a bitter attack on the company and, although Standard Oil claimed it was full of errors, no attempt to refute them was made because certain evils would have had to be admitted. Ida M. Tarbell's *History of the Standard Oil Company* began as a series of magazine articles in 1902 and appeared in book form in 1904. It was better documented than the Lloyd book, and Miss Tarbell accused Rockefeller and his associates of fraud and of having debased the business morality of the country. At the same time clergymen, politicians, and others were busy denouncing Rockefeller in print and by word of mouth. Standard Oil's very size was against it at a time when such giant industrial enterprises were new. It was the first major industrial monopoly and was the largest corporation in existence until the formation of United States Steel in 1901. Standard Oil was a marvelous organizational achievement. The quality of its products was high and its prices went down rather than up. The questions remain: Would prices have been even lower with more competition? And could the benefits of large-scale organization have been achieved with less reliance on shady practices?

For better or worse, the nation had to face the fact of the existence of powerful business units, far larger than any known before, in railroads, steel, oil, and other fields, including investment banking, which also became big business in this era.

10

The Men Who Made Money

The expansion of railroads, industry, and other businesses in the half century after the Civil War required large sums of money for construction, equipment, and raw materials. People and institutions with capital funds not needed for their own use were solicited to invest in the new and growing industries by buying stocks, or to lend money by buying bonds. Before the Civil War, most capital investment had been in the bonds of the federal government and state and local governments. The war gave further impetus to investment because of the large sums the Union government had to borrow and it also brought into the business of selling securities two new factors: the necessity of large-scale promotion to sell so many bonds and the further necessity to sell to the populace at large, not just to a few bankers or wealthy individuals.

When the railroads began to seek large sums by selling stocks and bonds, both the system for selling and the potential purchasers were available. Most of the money still came from incorporated or private banks and wealthy individuals. A great deal of investment money came from Europe where the longer history of nations and banks meant a larger accumulation of capital. By the 1870's, investment firms were forming syndicates to buy large bond or stock issues from, say, a railroad and to resell the securities in smaller units to individuals or foreign banks. This is known as underwriting. That investment banking itself became big business is reflected in the fact that by 1900 United States railroads had a total capitalization of $11.5 billion, while another $10 billion represented investments in manufacturing. Foreign investors held $3.3 billion of American securities, of which about $3 billion was in railroads. Clearly, banking was another lucrative field for the Robber Barons.

Two early investment bankers in the United States, who came from very different backgrounds, were August Belmont (1816–90) and Jay Cooke (1821–1905). Belmont was born in Germany and he translated his original name of Schonberg into Belmont when he moved to America. At the age of fourteen he went to work for the preeminent banking house of the Rothschild family in Frankfurt, and five years later he was confidential clerk to members of the family. In 1837 the firm sent him to Cuba to look into its loans there, but, coming by way of New York, Belmont arrived in America when the Panic of 1837 was at its height. He took it upon himself to stay in New York, straightening out the affairs of the Rothschild representative, and securing loans from Germany to prop up some New York banks that were near failure.

Belmont remained in America, opened his own investment firm and was the official Rothschild representative. In this position he was able to supply badly needed European capital for American railroads and other enterprises. His position gave him solid financial status which he used to secure social status as well, even though some people tried to hold his Jewish background against him. He took part in financial affairs with J. P. Morgan, but his main interests became politics and society. Belmont married the daughter of Commodore Matthew Calbraith Perry, who in 1854 opened Japan to the Western world. Active in Democratic party politics, Belmont was also strongly pro-Union in the Civil War and visited London and Paris to argue the Northern cause. He served as American minister to The Netherlands from 1853 to 1858. Belmont lived in grand style, collected art, and was an ardent horseman, serving as president of the American Jockey Club.

Jay Cooke came from an altogether different background and

made for himself a different career. Born in Ohio, he went to St. Louis, Missouri, when he was fifteen, worked there a few months, and then went to Philadelphia. He took a job in a banking house in 1839 and was made a junior partner at the age of twenty-one. In January 1861 he formed his own banking house and shortly attracted attention through his success in selling federal government bonds during the Civil War and because of the promotion methods in which he pioneered. Of the first $100 million loan in 1861, Cooke sold a quarter and the next year was named sole fiscal agent for the Treasury. By the end of the war in 1865, Cooke had sold about $2.5 billion of government bonds, using promotion methods that were new and startling. He had as many as five thousand agents working for him and he advertised widely. Cooke received a commission on the sales but paid all the expenses. Even so, his profit was considerable.

When peace came, Cooke was the best known banker in the country and he continued to handle government financing, although in 1873 he lost his monopoly when the Morgan interests fought for and got the right to manage half of a Treasury bond offering. Earlier, Cooke had adapted his war-bond methods to sell a Pennsylvania Railroad bond issue by forming a syndicate of eight firms to share the underwriting. Cooke's largest adventure in financing, and the one that led to his downfall, began at the start of 1870 when he became the sole financial agent for the Northern Pacific Railroad. Cooke foresaw large profits for himself and a great future for the line when it was finished. He was given control of three-fifths of the stock and was to receive a twelve per cent commission on bond sales, along with other benefits. He was also obligated to advance half a million dollars for immediate construction. As time went on, costs soared, the railroad's management was inept if not crooked, and the Cooke banking house by late 1872 had poured $5.5 million of its depositors' money into the Northern Pacific. With other railroad enterprises also overextended and the Crédit Mobilier scandal revealed to the public, the nation was heading for serious economic trouble. The Panic of 1873 was triggered in September of that year when Cooke's banking house had to close its doors and admit it was insolvent. The man who had been known as the Tycoon eventually paid all his debts, even selling his mansion to raise funds.

Later he invested a small amount of money in a silver mine which turned out so rich in ore that he sold his interest in 1879 for $1 million. Rich again, he bought back his mansion.

The greatest banker of them all, though, as almost everyone freely admitted, was John Pierpont Morgan (1837–1913), who achieved that eminence by the force of his personality as much as by the millions he controlled. Morgan was born in Hartford, Connecticut, on April 17, 1837, into a well-established and moderately well-to-do family. When his family moved to London in his youth, Morgan studied at a private school in Switzerland and then at the University of Göttingen in Germany. In 1856 he entered the banking firm in London of which his father was a partner. The firm was active in finding Europeans who wanted to invest capital in American enterprises. Morgan returned to the United States in 1857, worked for a time for a private bank but soon set up in business for himself as representative of George Peabody and Company, the firm with which his father was associated in London.

The young banker stayed out of the Civil War and hired a substitute in 1863 when conscription was instituted. During the war he also engaged in two business ventures which brought him considerable criticism in later years. In 1861 he loaned $20,000 to a man for a deal that became known as the Hall Carbine Affair. The borrower had a scheme for selling to General John C. Fremont for $22 each some carbines of an obsolete type that the War Department had previously disposed of for $3.50 each. There is no evidence either way as to whether or not Morgan knew what the deal was all about, but he did receive a commission for his services. The other incident involved speculation in gold in 1863. Morgan and another man quietly bought a quantity of gold in small amounts, then, with considerable fanfare, shipped half of it abroad. They hoped, correctly, that this would raise the price of gold in the United States. It did and they sold their remaining gold for a joint profit of $160,000. There was nothing illegal about the deal, nor even anything uncommon about it in that period, but it was hardly a patriotic thing to do. It depreciated, even if only temporarily, the value of the currency in a time of national emergency. In 1871, at the invitation of Anthony J. Drexel, a leading Philadelphia banker, Morgan became a partner in a New

York firm to be known as Drexel, Morgan and Company. The firm was immediately profitable.

Railroads offered the largest market for the services of investment bankers and so Morgan's new firm was quickly involved in their securities. In fact, a major part of Morgan's whole career concerned railroad securities and reorganizations. In 1879 William H. Vanderbilt, thinking to quiet public criticism by selling some of his family's enormous holdings in New York Central stock, arranged with Morgan to dispose of 150,000 shares directly to overseas purchasers, with an option for Morgan to sell another 100,000. The transaction was carried out successfully and so secretly that when the news broke in November it made a great impression on the rest of the financial community. Morgan at once became a leading financier, especially since he was now a director of the New York Central, representing the English investors to whom he had sold the stock.

Morgan's stature was apparent in 1885 when he acted as arbiter in a costly war between the Pennsylvania and the New York Central. The Pennsylvania's operators in 1885 decided to compete directly with the Central by taking over the bankrupt and uncompleted West Shore Railroad, which ran up the west side of the Hudson, parallel to the Central on the other bank. In retaliation, William H. Vanderbilt resolved to build a road across the state of Pennsylvania to compete with the line already there. He found Andrew Carnegie willing to invest $5 million in the project because of his displeasure with the way the Pennsylvania treated the freight shipments of his steel mills. Morgan could not stand to see such wasteful competition go on. If the plans were carried through, both roads would suffer. Accordingly, he called a meeting of those concerned, put them on board his yacht *Corsair*, and sailed them up and down the Hudson until they agreed to his proposal: the Central would take over the West Shore at a bargain price and would cease work on the new South Pennsylvania line. Peace was restored, railroad profits would not be damaged, and no one suffered except possibly small shippers who might have benefited from lower rates if the roads had had to compete for business.

Morgan also demonstrated his power and his determination in the case of the Philadelphia and Reading Railroad, whose finances he reorganized in the 1880's. A few years later a new president, A. Archibald McLeod, embarked on a program of expansion, trying to get a monopoly of the business of carrying anthracite coal, and purchasing interests in two New England lines. Morgan was outraged at what he considered improvidence but was defied by McLeod, who is reported to have said: "I would rather run a peanut stand than be dictated to by J. P. Morgan." Early in 1893 Drexel, Morgan began a raid on Reading stock, selling large quantities so as to depress the price. The line was forced into receivership and McLeod was removed from the presidency.

Morgan was opposed to the Interstate Commerce Act. He disliked any government interference in his affairs and he believed that cooperation among the railroads and more sensible financing would create an atmosphere in which railroads would prosper. Accordingly, he held several meetings in December 1888 and January 1889 at his home in New York. Present were the heads of all but two of the railroads west of Chicago and St. Louis, including Jay Gould and James J. Hill. After much discussion, during which Morgan promised not to finance the construction of competing rail lines if the roads would agree to avoid rate wars, the group adjourned. Like other such informal arrangements, however, it did not last long, indicating that where Morgan held the purse strings he could control events but that otherwise the railroad leaders were too individualistic to work together.

The Panic of 1893, despite the troubles it brought to investment bankers, also provided them, especially Morgan, with unusual opportunities for further tightening their grip on the nation's railroads. The overbuilding of the roads and the reckless measures taken to finance them were in themselves among the chief causes of the panic. The Interstate Commerce Commission reported that as of June 30, 1894, 192 railroads were in the hands of receivers as bankrupt. They represented 40,818 miles of track and $2.5 billion of capitalization, about a quarter of the total in each instance.

Morgan was called in by a number of railroads to reorganize their finances, and his methods followed a regular pattern. Bond issues were consolidated at a lower rate of interest; stockholders were heavily assessed to pay off accumulated debts; some of the bonds were replaced by stocks, which might or might not pay dividends sometime in the future. With these measures, a road might be sound again, at least for a while, but usually it had too much bonded debt and too much stock in relation to its assets. Morgan also insisted on having representation on and, in some cases, control of the board of directors for a certain number of years to keep a railroad management from getting into trouble again. As always, Morgan did whatever he could to keep railroads out of rate wars and other money-losing forms of competition.

To quite an extent, the public and investors accepted the reorganizations because Morgan's reputation stood behind them. He was able, for example, to create a relatively sound and practical Southern Railway Company from a jumble of thirty or so roads, holding companies, and subsidiaries in the Southeast. Morgan and his associates did not go unrewarded. For straightening out the affairs of the ailing Erie Railroad, he received a $500,000 fee and a commission on the new bonds issued. By 1898, Morgan had supervised the issuance of more than $1.5 billion of securities in the corporations he reorganized. He had strong financial influence on, if not control of, most of the railroads in the East and some in the West. By 1900, most of the important railroad mileage in the nation was controlled by half a dozen groups, including the so-called Morgan lines. He also exercised considerable influence in three of the other groupings.

Morgan's one costly failure in railroad reorganization came late in his career when he attempted to use the New York, New Haven and Hartford Railroad as the base for acquiring control of transportation in all of New England. In 1903 he brought in a new president of the line and encouraged him to expand and to buy out competition, such as steamships on Long Island Sound, interurban trolleys, and the Boston and Maine Railroad. Between 1903 and 1913 the New Haven's outstanding stocks and bonds rose from $93 million to $417 million. Shortly after Morgan died in 1913, his own firm stepped in to prevent further expenditures. The New Haven was unable to pay its usual dividend and it never again was strong financially.

Morgan did not confine his activities to railroads. He had an interest in a number of banks and had an active hand in organizing or reorganizing various industrial concerns. In 1892, with Henry

Villard, he merged the Edison General Electric Company and another firm to form the General Electric Company, which became the giant of that industry.

In the field of government finance, Morgan was instrumental in propping up the United States Treasury during the depression that followed the Panic of 1893. By late January 1895, the Treasury held only about half as much gold as was considered necessary. The panic had caused a loss of confidence in the dollar and under the law anyone could turn in paper currency and receive gold at face value. This had caused a drain on the Treasury's reserve. Morgan, with August Belmont and others, presented a plan to the government for restoring the gold reserve. After a good deal of discussion and much disagreement, Morgan suggested directly to President Cleveland a plan that would take advantage of a little known point in a law. Under this law, bonds could be issued to a group of bankers, rather than for public sale, and the Treasury would in turn receive gold coin, gathered in the United States and Europe. The bonds were issued and the plan worked. There was criticism, however, because private bankers made a profit out of their own government's difficulties. J. P. Morgan and Company (now the firm's name) profited to the extent of about a quarter of a million dollars and demonstrated that the bankers, not the government, held power over the nation's banking system and money supply.

Morgan first became interested in 1897 in the financial possibilities awaiting him in the steel industry. His initial venture was to put together, in collaboration with John W. Gates and others, an $80 million combination of steel and wire companies. The next year a combination of the Illinois Steel Company, an ore company and some other firms produced the Federal Steel Company, second in size only to Carnegie's. Other such combinations followed and eventually led to the scheme for merging the combinations, including the Carnegie interests, into the $1 billion United States Steel Corporation, as related in the chapter about Carnegie. When Morgan decided he wanted to include the Rockefeller property in the Mesabi Range to provide ore for United States Steel, he had to call on the elder Rockefeller in person after the latter declined to visit the banker. Later, John D., Jr., was sent to talk to Morgan and refused to be awed by him.

In the end, Henry Clay Frick acted as mediator between Morgan and Rockefeller and the latter received $5 million more for the ore property than Morgan first offered. As the great banker said: "In a business proposition as great as this would you let a matter of $5 million stand in the way of success?"

Success in steel was followed, however, by disaster in ocean shipping. Morgan conceived the idea of a consolidation of all the important British and American companies that sailed the Atlantic. As usual, one of his goals was to cut out competition that damaged profits and, of course, his firm would make money selling the stock of the new combine. Accordingly, he organized in 1902, six shipping companies with a combined fleet of one hundred twenty steamships into the International Mercantile Marine. The stock did not sell well, and the sinking of the *Titanic* in 1912, with a large loss of life after the ship hit an iceberg, hurt the reputation of the company. By 1914 it was bankrupt.

As the nineteenth century ended, the power of the bankers was not only becoming ever greater, but was being consolidated into cozy arrangements among investment banks, commercial banks, and insurance companies. The Morgan firm, for example, had what amounted to an alliance with the First National Bank of New York. Morgan also dominated the three large life insurance companies—the New York, the Equitable, and the Mutual—which by 1900 had invested the premiums of those they insured in about $1 billion of securities and other assets. One man, George W. Perkins, was both a partner in the Morgan firm and vice-president of the New York Life. The insurance companies had $50 million or more to invest each year. It was very profitable for the banks and bankers to have control over the insurance companies so that they could sell to them the new securities they poured out.

The Equitable Life numbered among those involved in its affairs not only Morgan but also Edward H. Harriman and Henry Clay Frick. The Equitable was founded in 1859 by Henry D. Hyde (1834–99) and by the time of his death had assets of over $250 million. He was succeeded by his son, James Hazen Hyde, only twenty-three at the time, whose extravagances as a party giver in society caused critical comment. For one ball he turned two floors of a restaurant into a replica of the palace of Versailles, and among the decorations were $28,500 worth of roses. Hyde was also involved with another faction in a struggle for control of the insurance company. Such criticism and turmoil, within and without, alarmed the bankers who wanted no attention called to one of the sources of their investment funds on which they made a great deal of money. The directors of Equitable appointed an investigating committee, headed by Henry Clay Frick, which recommended in May 1905 that Hyde and his rival both be removed from office.

By that time, newspapers had told the public enough to arouse a demand for an investigation of all insurance companies, which began in the fall of 1905. At its head was Charles Evans Hughes (1862–1948), who was given a start on a career that led him to the governorship of New York. Later he was the Republican candidate for president in 1916 and finally chief justice of the United States. Testimony at the hearings revealed that money paid in by policyholders, some of whom were quite poor, had been used to back political candidates, to buy favorable publicity, and to finance lobbying in Washington. The New York Life, with its close connection with the Morgan firm, had bought $4 million worth of the ill-fated International Mercantile Marine stock. Some reforms came out of the investigation, but a few years later Morgan was in firm control of the Equitable.

Morgan's last and most spectacular demonstration of his power over the nation's financial affairs took place in 1907. In that year a brief but severe financial panic struck, one that was sometimes referred to as a "rich man's panic." Although businessmen and bankers blamed it on President Theodore Roosevelt, who, they claimed, had interfered with business, it was clearly the result of too much speculation in the large money centers. Largely at fault were the trust companies who were not regulated enough to keep them from lending more money than their reserves justified. One damaging blow fell when a group of speculators who tried to corner the stock of a copper company failed and went bankrupt.

Morgan, in the fall of 1907, was seventy years old and no longer active in business on a full-time basis. When the crisis came he was in Richmond, Virginia, where he had gone to attend a convention of the Episcopal Church, taking with him several bishops in two special railroad cars. Upon returning to New York ahead of schedule, Morgan found that the Knickerbocker Trust Company was in trouble. In a few days, after a run on it by depositors, it exhausted its funds and had to close its doors. The Trust Company of America was also having difficulties, but Morgan believed it to be sound and he arranged for funds to support it. The elder Rockefeller put up $10 million to aid trust companies. The crisis, however, was not over. The Westinghouse Company failed and stock prices fell. The supply of currency ran low and Morgan had to raise $25 million to keep the New York Stock Exchange going. During the worst of the crisis, Morgan sat in a beautifully furnished room of his library on Thirty-sixth Street, playing solitaire while other bankers came and went with news and plans, seeking his approval as though he were tsar.

When it seemed as though the panic had been beaten, with such help as the United States Treasury could add to Morgan's efforts, a new problem arose when a leading brokerage firm threatened to collapse. The firm held a large amount of stock of the Tennessee Coal and Iron Company, which could not be converted into cash under the existing conditions. It was proposed that the United States Steel Corporation buy this stock and pay for it with its own very solid bonds. What, though, would President Roosevelt think if the giant of the steel industry took over another of its competitors? Frick and a steel company executive were sent overnight to Washington to find out. Just before the stock exchange was to open in New York the next day, they received the president's assurance that he would not treat the deal as a violation of the Sherman Antitrust Act. Once more Morgan had stemmed a potentially catastrophic crash of the nation's economy—but once more it had been shown that the banking system of the country was defective and that private bankers, in a pinch, wielded more power than the federal government.

While no one else in the American financial world approached Morgan in stature, two other bankers of the time also wielded great influence and often joined in Morgan's ventures. They were George F. Baker (1840-1931) and James Stillman (1850-1918). Like many of the other Robber Barons, Baker was a self-made man, beginning as a clerk, helping found the First

National Bank in 1863 and becoming president of it in 1877. Baker stayed in the background and worked willingly with Morgan, but, in fact, he was just as rich and almost as powerful. At one time he was a director of eighty-seven corporations. In 1908 he organized the First Security Company to buy and sell stock, which a commercial bank could not do.

Baker was known as the strong, silent man of Wall Street. He gave only one newspaper interview in his life and one time said: "It is none of the public's business what I do." In private life he was an art collector, with a sharp eye for values. He made many large gifts to such different institutions as the Washington Cathedral and the Harvard Business School, which his money founded. Nevertheless, when Baker died he was still worth about $73.5 million.

James Stillman, a Texan by birth, was also the silent type and like Baker exerted influence in the affairs of many companies. He was president of the National City Bank which, with Baker's bank, dominated the commercial banking scene in New York. A main source of Stillman's financial power was his alliance with the Rockefellers and other members of the Standard Oil group, especially William Rockefeller. (Stillman's two daughters married two of William Rockefeller's sons.) Earlier in his career, Stillman had been allied with Harriman against Hill and Morgan in the battle for control of western railroads. Gradually a community of interest developed among Morgan, Baker, and Stillman so that the three banking firms they controlled were all-powerful in their field. Stillman's estate was estimated to be worth $50 million when he died.

The power displayed and used by the men who controlled this concentration of money and credit led to increasing demands from political and civic leaders for an investigation of the "money trust," which appeared to be as monopolistic in its field as Standard Oil was in its. The result was the creation of the so-called Pujo Committee by the House of Representatives in early 1912. The committee took its name from Arsene P. Pujo (1861–1939), of Louisiana, who was chairman of the House Banking and Currency Committee. The star witness before the committee was Morgan, who seemed rather to enjoy himself once the proceedings got under way. He stoutly denied that he had any such overwhelming power as that attributed to him. He also denied that commercial credit was based primarily on money or property. "No, sir," he told the committee counsel, "the first thing is character. Before money or anything else. Money cannot buy it. . . . Because a man I do not trust could not get money from me on all the bonds in Christendom."

Baker also testified and was forced to admit that the concentration of control over money and credit had gone far enough. He even admitted that the country was not in a "comfortable situation" with so much concentration. When the investigation was over, the committee in its report went further and declared that "there is an established and well-defined identity and community of interest between a few leaders of finance . . . which has resulted in great and rapidly growing concentration of the control of money and credit in the hands of these few men." More specifically, the committee said this concentration had come about through the consolidation of banks that otherwise would have competed with each other, through interlocking directorates and stockholdings, and through the influence of the large investment bankers on insurance companies, railroads, and other industries. If the Morgan partners, the directors of the Baker and Stillman banks, plus the directors of two trust companies under Morgan influence were lumped together, they held among them 341 directorships in 112 corporations with resources of over $22 billion.

The work of the Pujo Committee and the report of a National Monetary Commission, which had already been investigating the banking system, resulted in the Federal Reserve Act of December 23, 1913. This law established twelve regional Federal Reserve Banks and a board in Washington to direct the entire system. National banks were required to belong to the system and, in effect, the reserve banks became bankers' banks. The banks issue Federal Reserve notes, while the member banks must keep a certain part of their deposits with the Reserve. The system brought about much greater coordination of the national banking system and put it under the control of the federal government. It made it possible to expand or contract the currency to meet business needs. While the Federal Reserve System did not destroy the power of bankers such as Morgan, it reduced it and, in principle, put the interests of the nation above those of the bankers.

J. P. Morgan was a rare combination of physical presence, personality, and financial power. He was a large man, six feet tall, with a square face. His black eyes were always described as fierce and penetrating. Dominating his face, though, was a huge purple nose, the result of a skin disease, but no one dared appear to notice it. As one railroad president said of him: "Wherever Morgan sits on a board is the head of the table even if he has but one share." Indeed, he had a kingly manner and all his life thought that the nation should be run by gentlemen such as himself.

Morgan lived luxuriously, even regally, with a home and several vacation places in the United States and two residences in England. He traveled extensively, usually spending several months a year in Europe. On one of his last trips he had a ship especially constructed to take him and his party up the Nile River. He also had his own yachts and the last one, *Corsair III*, built in 1898, was 302 feet long. When asked how much it cost to maintain such a yacht, Morgan replied, in effect: If you have to ask, you can't afford it. In 1906 he completed the building of the marble library on Thirty-sixth Street in New York to house his rare books and works of art. Morgan's son made the library a public institution in memory of his father in 1924. The financier knew almost everyone of importance, being a friend, for example, of both King Edward VII of Great Britain and Kaiser Wilhelm II of Germany.

The unofficial title of "most prominent layman of the Episcopal Church" was one Morgan could claim without dispute. He was senior warden of St. George's Church in New York and had its rector to breakfast every Monday to discuss parish affairs. He gave the church a new rectory and parish house and donated nearly $5 million toward the construction of the Cathedral of St. John the Divine. One of his favorite occupations was attending the conventions of the church, and at home he liked nothing better than to sing hymns on Sunday evening with family and friends.

A number of the Robber Barons turned to art collecting as their fortunes grew, but Morgan surpassed them all in the amount he spent and the number and variety of the items he gathered in. He spent about $60 million in all, paying, for example, $484,000 for an altarpiece by Raphael, $200,000 for a cup by Benvenuto Cellini, and $21,645 for a Louis XVI gold box. He was one of the founders of the Metropolitan Museum of New York in 1870 and became its president in 1904. When another collector failed to leave a valuable collection of Chinese porcelains to the Metropolitan in his will, as had been expected, Morgan bought the collection and presented it to the museum.

J. P. Morgan died in Rome on March 31, 1913. His estate, not counting the value of his art collection, was worth a relatively modest $68 million. Besides his contributions to the church, he had made many other large gifts during his lifetime, including money to the Harvard Medical School. The bulk of his estate and the art went to his son, also named John Pierpont. Eventually the Metropolitan received most of the works of art.

Unlike most of the other Robber Barons, Morgan never actually ran a railroad or managed a steel plant or other business or industrial enterprise. Yet he might be called the Robber Baron's Robber Baron for in him was summed up the basic power of all of them: the money and credit necessary to buy and control the railroads and manufacturing plants and to determine their policies and activities. These policies and activities in turn affected thousands of people, workers, and consumers as well as investors. And in that day and age such men were accountable only to their fellow bankers and industrial magnates—and to themselves.

11

The Gospel of Wealth

In medieval times the Robber Barons, from their castles commanding mountain passes and river crossings, levied tolls on merchants and others who needed to cross their territories. They performed no service and gave nothing in return for the privilege so that the toll they demanded amounted to robbery. In the 1880's and 1890's, the Populists and the Muckrakers revived the term to describe the men, among others, whose careers have been told in this book. Taking these men as a group, what were they like, and did they deserve so harsh a label?

They had a number of things in common, although whether these points of likeness account for their behavior cannot be proved. Of the fifteen men whose careers have been explored at some length—Carnegie, Crocker, Drew, Fisk, Frick, Gould, Harriman, Hill, Hopkins, Huntington, Morgan, Rockefeller, Stanford, Vanderbilt, and Villard—all had family heritages that were mostly northern European. Twelve of them were born on farms or in small towns; only Crocker, Morgan, and Villard entered the world in places that might be called more than villages. Carnegie and Villard were born abroad and Hill in Canada, but all three came to the United States when still young. The other twelve were all born in the northeastern United States—no fewer than eight in New York State, two in Connecticut, and one each in Pennsylvania and Vermont. None came from the South or West.

Only Morgan, Stanford, and Villard had anything resembling a college education, and Stanford was the only lawyer among them. Most of them enjoyed no more than the equivalent of an elementary school education, if that. Only Morgan and Villard came from families that were at all well-off. The parents of the others were either poor or in very modest circumstances. All but one left home at an early age to make their own living, usually starting out as farm hands, or store or office clerks. Only Morgan had the advantage of entering his father's business. All were hard workers, at least when young, and they began their advancement in the business world through their ability and their willingness to do what was necessary to get ahead. Of course, thousands of other young men left farms and small towns in these years because the only place to find business success beyond that of general storekeeper or village banker was in the old cities of the East or the new cities of the West. Four of the fifteen were among the thousands lured to California by the gold rush. Except for Drew and Vanderbilt, all were of military age when the Civil War began, but none of them served in uniform, although Hill tried to enlist but was rejected. All spent the war years making money and advancing their careers.

As they grew older, all except Fisk became average family men, so far as marriage and children were concerned. Again, except for Fisk, there was little or no scandal in the private life of any of the fifteen, although it was said of Morgan that "he collected beautiful women the way he collected art." They were mostly Protestant and active church members, although only Drew and Morgan were ostentatious in their religious activities. As they grew rich, they all spent considerable sums on luxurious living, but on the whole they did not flaunt their wealth as much as some others with less money and less reason to be proud of their careers. Fisk was the one great show-off so far as life-style was concerned and Crocker, Hopkins, and Stanford built residences as showy as any of the time. Harriman and Morgan, for example, lived just as well, but spent their money in quieter ways.

Most of them dabbled in some form of collecting as a way to spend their excess millions, but only Frick and Morgan built up magnificent collections. Carnegie and Rockefeller were, of course, the two greatest philanthropists by far, while others, such as Gould and Vanderbilt, gave away almost nothing in comparison with their wealth. Frick, Harriman, Hill, and Stanford were next after Carnegie and Rockefeller in the extent and good intentions of their giving. Only Drew died with his once large fortune gone, although Fisk had "only" a million dollars left when he was murdered. Gould, Harriman, Hill, Morgan, Rockefeller, and Vanderbilt had sons who, to some extent, carried on the family business after the death of the fathers. None of them showed the talent of the founder of the fortune, but, then, none of them had an opportunity to create his own career or fortune. Villard's son, Oswald Garrison Villard, became a leading journalist, following the path of his father's early career.

All fifteen of these Robber Barons were speculators in the sense that they all bought and sold stocks and bonds, sought to acquire real estate or other resources and raw materials that could be sold or exploited so as to yield a profit. In many of these activities they were gamblers, betting against others that some piece of paper would go up or down in value. In other situations, they held the equivalent of the medieval Robber Barons' river crossing and demanded an exorbitant price for whatever it was they had got hold of first. In none of these dealings were they doing anything constructive, nor were they adding to the real worth of the nation's resources and properties.

On the other hand, except for Drew, Fisk, and Gould, they all did do some constructive as well as some selfish and destructive things. At least half a dozen of them managed the construction and operation of railroads at a time when the nation wanted and needed them. Carnegie and Rockefeller oversaw the development of new and more efficient manufacturing processes. They built up new industries and pioneered in management methods that made such large-scale enterprises possible. Even Morgan supplied "raw materials" in the form of capital, without which industry could not have expanded. As speculators, the Robber Barons were parasites taking advantage of the system. Those who were also producers were establishing the base of the American economic system that still exists today, with modifications brought about by public opinion and government controls.

The primary place of railroads in the American economy during this period is indicated by the fact that eleven of these Robber Barons, not counting Morgan as railroad financier, made their careers and fortunes as railroad builders or manipulators, or both. It can, however, be argued that the business of such a man as Drew was dealing in railroad securities, not in transportation.

Americans in general felt two ways about the railroads. They wanted and needed them to move settlers to the West, to carry finished goods from east to west, and to bring eastward the food and other raw materials needed in the cities. Railroads were the first and greatest symbols of the new age of powerful machines. Americans admired the speed and the strength of the locomotives, the romance of faraway places they hinted of as they whistled, belched black smoke, and roared on to some distant destination. Many people invested their small savings in railroads to help bring the iron rails to their small home town. They also voted to invest tax money in railroad bonds and they approved of grants of public land. Their disappointment, frustration, and anger were all the greater when they found freight rates were set arbitrarily high to make them pay all that could be squeezed out of them, or when their stocks and bonds lost value because the roads had been milked of millions of dollars by dishonest builders and speculators. The railroad owners and managers had only themselves to blame when the American people began to demand government regulation.

Still, the people could not help but admire the technological achievement the railroad tracks represented and be awed by the power the railroad magnates represented. James Bryce wrote in *The American Commonwealth:*

> *These railroad kings are among the greatest men, perhaps I may say are the greatest men, in America. They have wealth, else they could not hold the position. They have fame, for everyone has heard of their achievements; every newspaper chronicles their movements. They have power, more power—that is more opportunity of making their personal will prevail—than perhaps anyone in political life, except the President and the Speaker, who after all hold theirs only for four years and two years, while the railroad monarch may keep his for life.*

It is doubtful that Drew ever felt the need of any philosophy or social theory to justify his business methods and his outlook on life, but more thoughtful men, such as Carnegie, were anxious to find intellectual support for what they were doing during business hours. They found it in Social Darwinism, which was based on an analogy with Charles Darwin's theory of evolution. Darwin's theory said that there was a process of natural selection during which, in a struggle for existence, the organisms best adapted to the environment survived while others perished. Applied to economic life, the theory said that economic competition was the same as biological competition in the world of nature. Those who survived this struggle and became rich and powerful deserved to and the fact that they survived meant they were superior. The poor were poor because they were less fit for the struggle. Poverty was an evil, but necessary because if one tried to interfere with it one was interfering with the laws of nature. Society should accept the poverty of some as part of the overall arrangement of society which would, eventually, improve because the evolutionary process went ever upward. In the meantime, poverty was to be made less burdensome by the Christian charity of those who had made good in the never-ending struggle.

In Great Britain, Herbert Spencer (1820–1903) wrote voluminously in support of Darwin and became the leading exponent there of Social Darwinism. Carnegie thought highly of Spencer and tried to make the shy intellectual more of a public figure. He managed to entice Spencer to come to the United States in 1882 and saw to it that he was guest of honor at a dinner which was attended by most of the important figures in the world of business and finance.

In America, the two leading popularizers of Social Darwinism were John Fiske (1842–1901) and William Graham Sumner (1840–1910). Fiske, both a philosopher and a historian, was popular as a lecturer and his histories were widely read. His main intellectual effort, however, was to try to reconcile the commonly accepted religious beliefs of the time with science as expounded by Darwin and Spencer.

Sumner was an Episcopal clergyman as well as a sociologist and political economist, who taught at Yale University after 1872.

He was against any interference whatsoever by government in economic affairs. He contended that nothing could change the natural customs that had evolved. His best known work was *What Social Classes Owe to Each Other* (1883), in which he wrote:

> *The yearning after equality is the offspring of envy and covetousness, and there is no possible plan for satisfying that yearning which can do aught else than rob A to give to B; consequently all such plans nourish some of the meanest vices of human nature, waste capital, and overthrow civilization. But if we can expand the chances we can count on a general and steady growth of civilization and advancement of society by and through its best members. In the prosecution of these chances we all owe to each other good-will, mutual respect, and mutual guarantees of liberty and security. Beyond this nothing can be affirmed as a duty of one group to another in a free state.*

To Sumner, of course, the "best members" of society were such men as Carnegie and Morgan. "Good-will" and "mutual guarantees" meant that such men were free to do as they wished in economic affairs, without any control by government.

Not everyone among the intellectual leaders of the nation agreed with Sumner. Two of those who did not were Charles Francis Adams and Henry Adams (1838–1928), brothers whose grandfather and great-grandfather had been presidents of the United States. Charles Francis, in particular, spoke from practical—and unhappy—experience in the railroad field. A combat veteran of the Civil War, from which he emerged as a brigadier general, he turned to the railroad system because he felt it was "the most developing force and largest field of the day." Articles he wrote on the railroad situation secured him a place on the Massachusetts Railroad Commission, which was established in 1869 and was the first regulatory board of its kind. That same year, *Chapters of Erie*, by Charles Francis and Henry, which was extremely critical of both the recent war for control of the Erie and of the Gold Conspiracy, was published. Charles Francis was chairman of the Massachusetts Railroad Commission from 1872 to 1879. His railroad activities then became more extensive; in 1882 he was elected a director of the Union Pacific and two years later, president. The road was in a bad way and Adams believed that he did much to improve and restore its operations. He admitted in his autobiography, however, that he later displayed "indecision and weakness," but he was most unhappy when he was "ejected" by Jay Gould in 1890. The aristocratic Charles Francis Adams was, therefore, prejudiced when he wrote in his autobiography:

I have known, and known tolerably well, a good many "success-ful" men—"big" financially—men famous during the last half century; and a less interesting crowd I do not care to encounter. Not one that I have ever known would I care to meet again, either in this world or the next; nor is one of them associated in my mind with the idea of humor, thought or refinement. A set of mere money-getters and traders, they were essentially unattrac-tive and uninteresting. The fact is that money-getting, like everything else, calls for a special aptitude and great concentra-tion. . . .

Henry Adams, historian, scholar, and editor, took no part in business affairs and the older he grew, the more distaste he expressed for contemporary American political and economic life. When two leading British periodicals turned down an article on the Gold Conspiracy, he was shocked and thought the editors were afraid of the power of Gould and others involved. A third magazine eventually published it. In his autobiography, *The Education of Henry Adams*, which was not published until about six months after his death in 1918, he wrote of the railroad era: "The generation between 1865 and 1895 was already mortgaged to the railways, and no one knew it better than the generation itself." Of the Robber Barons he echoed his brother's somewhat snobbish view: "The men who commanded high pay were as a rule not ornamental. Even Commodore Vanderbilt and Jay Gould lacked social charm."

Others did not entirely agree with the opinion that all the Robber Barons were dislikable and disliked by the whole nation. James Bryce thought that "the feeling of the American public toward the very rich is, so far as a stranger can judge, one of curiosity and wonder rather than respect." A character in William Dean Howells's novel, *A Hazard of New Fortunes* (1889), asserts that the successful financier and speculator was "the ideal and ambition of most Americans." In another ten years another novelist, Henry James, wrote that millionaires had become "the typical American figure."

Since there were no public opinion polls at the time, it is impossible to say how many Americans admired the Robber Barons and how many did not. Certainly, the Civil War sped up a trend that took attention away from politics and politicians and focused it more and more on businessmen. Many Americans may have disapproved of the methods of the new millionaires and of the way they flaunted their wealth. Nevertheless, thousands of Americans tried as hard as they could to join the favored group. Only fortune or their own actions prevented them from rising to the top, too. As the years went on, resentment against the Robber Barons for their actions as railroad manipulators or controllers of trusts that overcharged the consumer increased. It found expression in books, magazine articles, and editorials, and later in the passage of laws designed to control the power of these men.

Much resentment was expressed against individual Robber Barons while they were alive. Carnegie was denounced for his part in the violent Homestead strike, while John D. Rockefeller, Sr., was at one time said to be the most hated man in America. The public, however, was just as quick to forgive and forget. Before he died, Rockefeller was looked upon as a kindly, very old man who handed out dimes right and left. After his many philanthropic acts, Carnegie was referred to in one case, at least, as "St. Andrew," while Pope Pius X called Morgan "a great and good man."

What can be said in defense of the Robber Barons? Time has given a different perspective and they are not now so harshly denounced as they were in the days of the Muckrakers. They lived in a period when the growth of the country and the advance of technology made it inevitable that more railroads would be built and that industrial processes would expand tremendously. That was the direction in which the world had been moving ever since the beginning of the Industrial Revolution in Great Britain about a hundred years earlier.

Those men did what others would have done if they had had the opportunity. They performed more efficiently tasks in the economic world that someone was certain to do sooner or later. The poor but helpful miner panning for a little gold in California gave no more thought to the welfare of his competitors or the damage he might be doing to the environment than did Rockefeller or Carnegie in their larger affairs. Those who take the most sympathetic view of the men and their times think of them as "industrial statesmen," which seems going a bit far. The fact remains, though, that some of them at least took pride in their products and their organization. Carnegie insisted on producing the best steel at the lowest price and Rockefeller could claim correctly that no refinery offered better products than those of Standard Oil. Such an attitude is, in the long run anyway, a profitable one, but both these men could probably have made just as much money if they had produced goods of a lower quality. What is most difficult to overlook today is the inhuman way in which labor was treated—the long hours of work, the low pay, and the refusal to deal with organized workers as equals.

Perhaps neither "industrial statesmen" nor Robber Barons is the right term to apply to this group of unusual men. The medieval barons were small-scale extortionists, whereas men such as Carnegie operated on a much larger scale and were, in their fields, empire builders. In his biography of Carnegie, Andrew Frazier Wall suggests that if such men of the nineteenth century are to be related to the historic past, then

> given their temperament and ambition, men like Carnegie and Rockefeller deserve to be assigned the more illustrious—or more infamous—roles of Charlemagne, Tamerlane, or Suleiman the Magnificent. Of course they were wasteful of men and resources, as much so as any conqueror building an empire by military force. They were as self-centered as Alexander or Caesar. Their historical perspective, as it related to industrial development, was always from a personal point of view, not from a societal or even a national one. . . . Their own empire comprised as much of the economic world as their entrepreneurial statemanship could encompass.

For Further Reading

ADAMS, CHARLES FRANCIS. *Charles Francis Adams, 1835–1915: An Autobiography.* Boston: Massachusetts Historical Society, 1916. (Reprinted in 1968 by Russell & Russell.)

———, and ADAMS, HENRY. *Chapters of Erie.* Ithaca: Cornell University Press, 1956. (Originally published in 1869.)

ALLEN, FREDERICK LEWIS. *The Great Pierpont Morgan.* New York: Harper & Bros., 1949.

———. *The Lords of Creation.* New York: Harper & Bros., 1935. (Paperback edition published by Quadrangle Books, 1966.)

ANDREWS, WAYNE. *The Vanderbilt Legend: The Story of the Vanderbilt Family, 1794–1940.* New York: Harcourt, Brace & Co., 1941.

BOARDMAN, FON W., JR. *America and the Civil War Era, 1850–1875.* New York: Henry Z. Walck, Inc., a division of David McKay Co., 1976.

———. *America and the Gilded Age, 1876–1900.* New York: Henry Z. Walck, Inc., 1972.

———. *America and the Progressive Era, 1900–1917.* New York: Henry Z. Walck, Inc., 1970.

BROWN, DEE. *Hear That Lonesome Whistle Blow: Railroads in the West.* New York: Holt, Rinehart & Winston, 1977.

CARNEGIE, ANDREW. *Autobiography of Andrew Carnegie.* Boston and New York: Houghton Mifflin Co., 1920.

———. *The Gospel of Wealth.* New York: Century Co., 1900. (Reprinted in 1962 by Harvard University Press.)

COCHRAN, THOMAS C., and MILLER, WILLIAM. *The Age of Enterprise.* Rev. ed. New York: Harper & Row, 1961.

COLLIER, PETER, and HOROWITZ, DAVID. *The Rockefellers: An American Dynasty.* New York: Holt, Rinehart & Winston, 1976. (Paperback edition published by New American Library, Inc., 1977.)

COREY, LEWIS. *The House of Morgan: A Social Biography of the Masters of Money.* New York: G. Howard Watt, 1930.

DULLES, FOSTER RHEA. *Labor in America.* 3rd ed. New York: Thomas Y. Crowell Co., 1966.

ECKENRODE, H. J., and EDMUNDS, POCAHONTAS WIGHT. *E. H. Harriman: The Little Giant of Wall Street.* New York: Greenberg, Inc., 1933.

FAULKNER, HAROLD UNDERWOOD. *American Economic History.* 8th ed. New York: Harper & Row, 1960.

FLYNN, JOHN T. *God's Gold: The Story of Rockefeller and His Times.* New York: Harcourt, Brace & Co., 1932.

FULLER, ROBERT H. *Jubilee Jim: The Life of Colonel James Fisk, Jr.* New York: The Macmillan Co., 1928.

GRODINSKY, JULIUS. *Jay Gould, His Business Career, 1867–1892.* Philadelphia: University of Pennsylvania Press, 1957.

HACKER, LOUIS M. *The Shaping of the American Tradition.* Vol. 2. New York: Columbia University Press, 1947.

HARVEY, GEORGE. *Henry Clay Frick, The Man.* New York: Charles Scribner's Sons, 1928. (A privately printed edition in 1936.)

HEDGES, JAMES BLAINE. *Henry Villard and the Railways of the Northwest.* New Haven: Yale University Press, 1930. (Reprinted in 1967 by Russell & Russell.)

HENDRICK, BURTON J. *The Life of Andrew Carnegie.* 2 vols. Garden City: Doubleday & Co., 1932. (Reprinted in 1969 by Harper & Row.)

HOLBROOK, STEWART H. *James J. Hill.* New York: Alfred A. Knopf, 1955.

HOYT, EDWIN P. *The Goulds, A Social History.* New York: Weybright & Talley, Inc., 1969.

JOHNSON, ALLEN, ed. *Dictionary of American Biography.* 22 vols. New York: Charles Scribner's Sons, 1928–1974.

JOSEPHSON, MATTHEW. *The Robber Barons: The Great American Capitalists, 1861–1901.* New York: Harcourt, Brace & World, Inc., 1962. (Paperback reprint of 1934 edition.)

KATZ, IRVING. *August Belmont: A Political Biography.* New York: Columbia University Press, 1968.

KENNAN, GEORGE. *E. H. Harriman: A Biography.* 2 vols. Boston and New York: Houghton Mifflin Co., 1922.

KIRKLAND, EDWARD C. *Dream and Thought in the Business Community, 1860–1900.* Ithaca: Cornell University Press, 1956. (Paperback edition published by Quadrangle Books, 1964.)

————. *Industry Comes of Age: Business, Labor, and Public Policy, 1860–1897.* New York: Holt, Rinehart & Winston, Inc., 1961. (Paperback edition published by Quadrangle Books, 1967.)

LANE, WHEATON J. *Commodore Vanderbilt: An Epic of the Steam Age.* New York: Alfred A. Knopf, 1942.

LARSON, H. M. *Jay Cooke, Private Banker.* Cambridge, Mass.: Harvard University Press, 1936. (Reprinted in 1968 by Greenwood Press.)

LAVENDER, DAVID. *The Great Persuader.* Garden City, N.Y.: Doubleday & Co., 1970. (A biography of Collis P. Huntington.)

LEWIS, OSCAR. *The Big Four: The Story of Huntington, Stanford, Hopkins and Crocker, and of the Building of the Central Pacific.* New York: Alfred A. Knopf, 1966.

MARTIN, ALBRO. *James J. Hill and the Opening of the Northwest.* New York: Oxford University Press, 1976.

MORGAN, H. WAYNE, ed. *The Gilded Age: A Reappraisal.* Syracuse, N.Y.: Syracuse University Press, 1963.

NEVINS, ALLAN. *John D. Rockefeller.* 1 vol. abridgement of *Study in Power.* New York: Charles Scribner's Sons, 1959.

NORRIS, FRANK. *The Octopus.* New York: New American Library, Inc., 1964. (Originally published in 1901.)

O'CONNOR, RICHARD. *Gould's Millions.* Garden City, N.Y.: Doubleday & Co., 1962. (Reprinted in 1973 by Greenwood Press.)

PYLE, JOSEPH GILPIN. *The Life of James J. Hill.* 2 vols. Garden City, N.Y.: Doubleday & Co., 1916. (Reprinted in 1968 by Peter Smith.)

STOVER, JOHN F. *American Railroads.* Chicago: University of Chicago Press, 1961.

SWANBERG, W. A. *Jim Fisk: The Career of an Improbable Rascal.* New York: Charles Scribner's Sons, 1959.

TARBELL, IDA M. *History of the Standard Oil Company.* Briefer version. New York: Harper & Row, 1966. (Paperback edition published by W. W. Norton, Inc., 1969.)

TUTOROW, NORMAN E. *Leland Stanford: Man of Many Careers.* Menlo Park, Ca.: Pacific Coast Publishers, 1971.

TWAIN, MARK, and WARNER, CHARLES DUDLEY. *The Gilded Age.* Seattle: University of Washington Press, 1968. (Corrected edition, originally published in 1873.)

VILLARD HENRY. *Memoirs of Henry Villard, Journalist and Financier, 1835–1900.* 2 vols. Boston and New York: Houghton Mifflin Co., 1904. (Reprinted in 1969 by DaCapo Press.)

WALL, JOSEPH FRAZIER. *Andrew Carnegie.* New York: Oxford University Press, 1970.

WARSHOW, ROBERT IRVING. *Jay Gould: The Story of a Fortune.* New York: Greenberg, Inc., 1928.

WHEELER, GEORGE. *Pierpont Morgan and Friends: The Anatomy of a Myth.* Englewood Cliffs, N.J.: Prentice-Hall, Inc., 1973.

WHITE, BOUCK. *The Book of Daniel Drew.* New York: George H. Doran Co., 1910.

WINKLER, JOHN K. *Morgan the Magnificent.* New York: Vanguard Press, 1930.

Index